WALKS IN THE HILLS OF KENT

Walks in the Hills of Kent

JANET SPAYNE & AUDREY KRYNSKI

of The Ramblers Association
Croydon & District Group

SPURBOOKS LIMITED

Published by:
SPURBOOKS LIMITED
6 Parade Court
Bourne End
Buckinghamshire

© Janet Spayne & Audrey Krynski 1976

Sketch Maps by Mike Pocock

At the time of publication all but two of the footpaths used in these walks were designated as official footpaths, but it should be borne in mind that diversion orders may be made from time to time.

I S B N   O 904978 14 1

Contents

Introduction

WE were pleasantly surprised at the evident popularity of "Walks in the Surrey Hills" but from our many encounters with users of the book we have come to realise that most ordinary people enjoy that most natural pursuit—walking in the countryside. They may feel hesitant about undertaking a walk unaided, but written instructions give confidence and the reassurance that they will find their way back to where the car was parked without walking an inordinate number of miles.

The work entailed in writing this book of rambles has proved most enjoyable and has extended our existing knowledge of Kent. We have confined our exploration to an area of Kent easily accessible from the metropolitan suburbs. This beautiful area of Kent offers a great variety of landscape: wooded hills and little secluded valleys, open downland, forestry areas which are pleasing to the eye, rivers, lakes— mostly man-made but none the less attractive for that—farmlands, hopfields, orchards, historic buildings and domestic architecture of bygone centuries.

In compiling this book we had principally in mind the ordinary family walking together, and the rambles are therefore short, but a glance at the sketch maps will show that it is often possible to link two walks together to make a longer ramble. With each walk the appropriate O.S. 1:50,000 map number is given and similarly the number of the 2½" map which, though not essential, gives greater detail. For normal use the sketch map for each walk will be adequate.

It is accepted that everyone needs recreation and a change from the everyday round. Ruling out expensive holidays, walking practically on one's own doorstep could well provide recreation in the true sense of the word. Furthermore it will benefit mind and body as we discover that simple pleasures are the most rewarding.

AUDREY KRYNSKI

JANET SPAYNE

Westerham

**Farley Common, High Chart, The Chart,
Crockham Hill Common, Mariners Hill,
Squerryes Park. 7 miles
Mariners Hill. 6 miles**

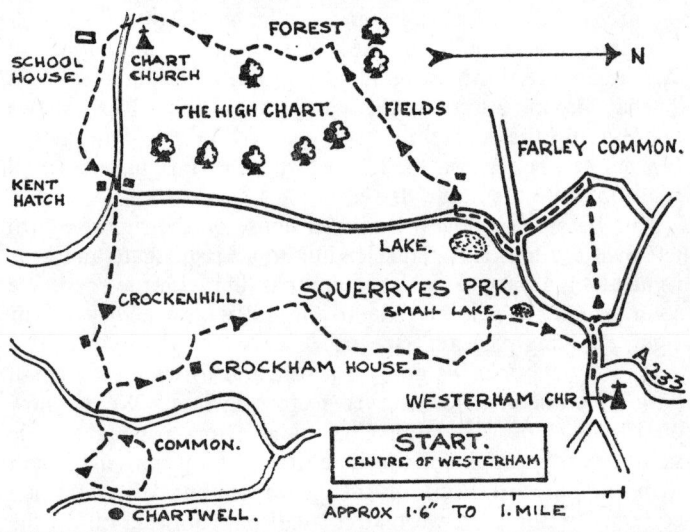

THIS is a walk through parkland and open woodland, with an opportunity to visit Chartwell. In May there will be bluebells in many of the woods and in June the rhododendrons are a fine sight. This walk is best done in winter or spring, before the trees are in full leaf. There will be some mud but most of it can be avoided.

How to get there: Buses 410, 483 (not Sundays), 485 (not Sundays). Green Line 705 and 706. By car on the A.25 or A.233. There is a free car park just off the A.233.

We leave the centre of Westerham turning right on the road signposted Tatsfield and Croydon and immediately left through posts down a tarmac path leading into Westbury Terrace. A short distance forward and uphill brings us to a signposted footpath between hedges which we follow till it brings us out on to Farley Common where we continue direction on a tarmac drive with a grass area on our right. We are soon at a road where we turn left, cutting off the corner by taking a small path down on the left. In less than a quarter of a mile we are at the main road where we turn left for a few yards then right on another road passing on our left a picturesque row of cottages and the lodge of Squerryes Park, a manor house built in 1681 and open to the public on Wednesdays, Saturdays, Sundays and Bank Holidays between 2 and 6 p.m. Admission 25p, Gardens only, 15p. As we continue up the road the Squerryes Park lake and the house beyond can be seen on the left before we turn right on a small road opposite the house drive.

Just before reaching a timbered house on the right we turn left over a ditch on a plank leading to a kissing gate and bear right along a narrow field keeping parallel with the road. We soon go over a stile and slightly uphill with a hedge on our right, enjoying pleasant aspects.

As the field ends we go over a stile and forward on a small path which soon takes us over a crossing track. We are now on the edge of The High Chart and after crossing a wide sandy forestry track we continue direction on our small path with the upward slope of the heath on our left. At some conifers on our right we take a small path forking off on the left and are soon out on a wide track near a junction of paths with the road close by on our right.

Here we take the third track on our left leading us uphill to a wide forestry track where we turn right and continue forward ignoring side turnings. We are now on the highest part of High Chart and can enjoy good views. After bearing left our track is joined by another track coming in on the right and we bear right to take a small easily missed path immediately on the left of the joining track, taking us into trees and soon across a small stream and uphill. The source of this stream is just off to the left and after a rainy season gushes clearly from the foot of a small bank. We continue

8

forward and soon after the path flattens out we turn left on a rather indistinct crossing path leading us at once to a main track where we turn left for a few yards then right on a small path between young pine trees. Ignoring a left fork we go forward through an area of old quarries giving rise to many dips and embankments, continuing to a crossing track where we turn right then left around a hollow full of pine trees on our left. We soon turn right on a crossing track by a pine on a "table" base, using good mud avoidance paths on the left where necessary. When we are nearly out to the open heath ahead our path forks and we keep left, finally coming out to the road. If refreshment is needed The Carpenters Arms is across the road and straight ahead on the right.

If we are not visiting the inn, we turn left down the road, passing the Limpsfield Chart church before we cross the main road to a signposted bridleway initially with a tarmac surface and, opposite an old schoolhouse, bearing left into trees. Our track takes us through pleasant open beechwoods with an upward slope on our left and a view down on our right when the trees are not in full leaf. Later we have a larch plantation on our right and though these trees have greatly increased in height in recent years there are gaps which afford good views to the south. After crossing a tarmac drive our track goes steeply uphill and turns sharply to the left at the top but we continue forward on a well defined path into trees, soon passing on our right the back of a house built on the hillside. Here we bear left on a surfaced drive and after passing a gap in the trees on the right where the North Sea gas pipe was laid—now fortunately planted with rhododendrons—we are soon out at the road where we turn right for a short distance passing Kent Hatch house on our right.

We cross the road to a seat just past a small road turning off on the left and take a signposted footpath which at first keeps parallel with the main road. After occasional mud avoidance paths at the side we keep left at a fork just after a prominent avoidance rejoins the main path and continue through pleasant open woods of Crockham Hill Common, later going over a crossing track. Another path feeds in on the left and we are soon at a junction of paths where we take

9

the second on the right, i.e. straight ahead. We are now in an area of silver birch and scattered pine trees and finally emerge in a clearing in front of a house, The Warren. With the house on our right we ignore the first path turning off diagonally on the right and take the next path with a holly bush on the right, soon bearing slightly left through silver birches. We are joined by a path coming in on either side and continue downhill through woods. At the bottom of the hill our path merges with two other paths from left and right and a short distance on an uphill drive brings us to the road. The walk may be shortened here by omitting Mariners Hill and Chartwell.

For the longer version
We cross the road to a footpath opposite on the right of a private drive and go steeply uphill. After passing a house and fence on our right we keep to the footpath on the extreme right with the open space of Mariners Hill on our right. Just before our path bears left and goes steeply downhill to the road opposite Chartwell we turn left on a slightly rising path taking us into an area of rhododendrons.

If we wish to visit Chartwell, the former home of Sir Winston Churchill, now in the care of the National Trust, we continue down to the road and retrace our steps to pick up the walk later. Chartwell is open to the public on Saturdays, Sundays, Mondays, Wednesdays and Thursdays also Bank Holidays during the summer months. Admission 50p, Gardens only 20p.

Having turned left we stay on this path for about a quarter of a mile and when the trees are not in full leaf it is possible to see Chartwell down on our right and Toys Hill beyond. We finally emerge from the rhododendrons into a more open area with a slope down on our right and after turning sharply left slightly uphill we keep to the centre main path when it immediately forks on both sides. Another fork almost at once is only a mud avoidance diversion and soon rejoins the original path. Later, at a definite fork we keep left on the narrower path and soon finding ourselves opposite the garden

10

fence we passed earlier, we turn right down the drive to the road.

Both walks now follow the same route

We cross to the April Cottage drive opposite and go downhill to a junction of paths where we take the one on the extreme right and continue for about a quarter of a mile with the slopes of Crockham Hill Common rising on our left. Some parts of this path are decidedly muddy but there are good mud avoidance paths at a slightly higher level on our left. Just past the garden of Crockham House on our right we turn right over a stile and go forward over an uneven meadow to another stile with a wooded hill with ancient earthworks on our left. With a wire fence on our left we continue through this pleasant valley along a small ridge enjoying fine views ahead. Another stile brings us into Squerryes Park and we go forward for a short distance then turn right with a wire fence on our left, finally bearing left through a wire barrier. We now continue on a grassy track through meadows for nearly three quarters of a mile, following the line of the River Darent on our right beyond which rise the wooded slopes of Tower Wood.

When Westerham comes into sight ahead our track bears slightly left to a lodge and a stile which takes us on to a rough drive where we continue past a small lake on our left and the river on our right. Just past a small bridge our our right we bear right on a path passing a beautiful cottage on our left and going uphill to a stile we are soon out at a small road. We cross to an enclosed footpath opposite which finally turns left through the Kings Arms car park and brings us to a bus stop in the main road of Westerham, opposite the George and Dragon.

Refreshment: Westerham where there are several inns and tea shops and at Limpsfield Chart where there is an inn.

Westerham

Tower Wood, Mariners Hill, Crockham Hill
High Chart. $7\frac{1}{4}$ miles
Tower Wood, Squerryes Park. $3\frac{3}{4}$ miles

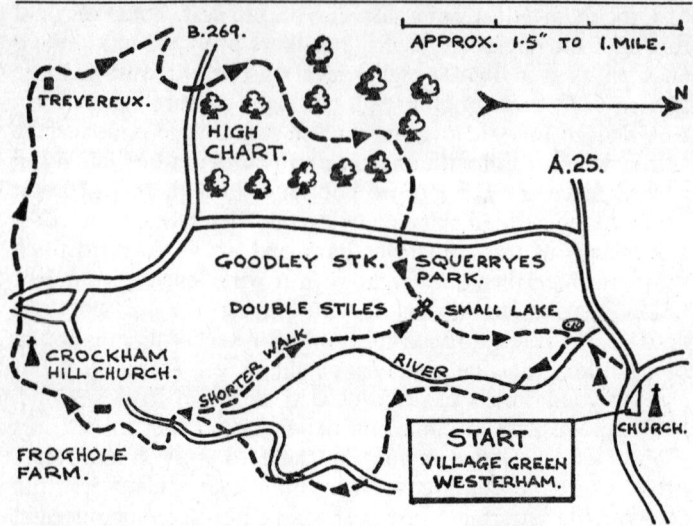

HERE we have delightful woodland walking with fine views varied with some field walking. There will be bluebells in late spring, heather in August, but above all this is a walk to appreciate autumn colour: the red turkey oaks and golden silver birch in October look splendid against a dark background of conifers. The field paths are bound to be muddy in winter and early spring.

How to get there: Buses 410, 483 (not Sundays), 485 (not Sundays). Green Line 705 and 706. By car on the A.25 or A.233 or B.2024. There is a free car park just off the A.233.

With our backs to the green at Westerham we turn down Water Lane, at the end of which we turn right along the bottom of sloping meadows. A footbridge takes us over the

River Darent in its early stages and we turn left along a small road to a lodge on our right where we go over a stile and bear left along a track, following the line of the river down on our left among trees. After 300 yards or so we go through a gate, turn left down to another gate, over the stream on an earth bridge and immediately turn right over a barrier on to a small path at the edge of Tower Wood. We stay on this very pleasant path for about half a mile with a steep upward slope on our left and, later, open aspects on our right. Just after the path touches the stream it turns left uphill through conifers bringing us to a T junction where we go right keeping along the contour. When our path bears left and forks we turn sharply left uphill and when it forks again almost at once, we still go left and uphill, enjoying fine views on our right. At the top of the hill we go forward to a ruined tower in an open space from where we can see the North Downs on our left. Here we turn right along a wide grassy track which soon bears left and out to the road which we cross to posts and a small path taking us into a wooded area known as Horns Hill.

Soon after entering the wood we turn right and follow a white waymarked path which twists and turns more or less parallel with the road eventually coming out into the road where we turn left. Very soon at a road junction we continue forward on the road signposted to Edenbridge and a few yards past the end of the railings on the left we turn left on a small uphill path into woods, mainly beech. At the top of the hill we go over a crossing track and downhill through bracken to the road which we cross to a signposted footpath opposite. This takes us steeply downhill to a path at a lower level where we turn left continuing parallel with the road through a strip of woods. When we come to a major track we have the choice of a longer or shorter walk.

For the shorter version
At the major track we turn right for about a quarter of a mile to Crockham House on the right behind a high fence. Some parts of this path are decidedly muddy but there are good mud avoidance paths at a slightly higher level on our

left. Just past the house we turn right over a stile and go forward over an uneven meadow to another stile with a wooded hill with ancient earthworks on our left. With a wire fence on our left we continue through this pleasant valley along a small ridge enjoying fine views ahead. Another stile brings us into Squerryes Park and we go forward, ignoring a track which turns right towards the River Darent and Tower Wood, and take an uphill path with a wire fence on our right. Our track bears left at the top of the hill and at a point where we have stiles on both sides we turn right.

For the longer version
At the major track we turn left and bear left again out to the road. We cross the road going through posts to a steep footpath opposite and on reaching a garden fence at the top of the slope we turn sharply back on our right, keeping right when the path forks and following the line of the road which is down on our right. Our path bears right and continues with a wire fence and the open space of Mariners Hill on our left and distant views of the South Downs. We can make a pleasant diversion by turning left with the wire fence and continuing on to a stile on our left which will take us over to a memorial stone indicating that the area was given to The National Trust in 1904. Opposite the stile is a small path leading to a memorial seat set in a splendid position on the steep hillside and giving fine views to the south with Crockham Hill church in the foreground. The church is Victorian Gothic and contains the tomb of the famous Octavia Hill, one of the founders of The National Trust.

Retracing our steps to the corner of the wire fence, we turn left downhill and down steps to the road where we turn left through a gate down Froghole Lane, passing picturesque Froghole Farm on our right. As the lane bears left at an oast house we turn right down a signposted footpath going down steps which take us through an area of beautiful hillside cottages and gardens. After going over a stile we continue downhill with a hedge on our right, cross a bridge over a stream and another stile and continue over the centre of the field bearing slightly left, later passing Crockham Hill church-

14

yard over on our right. Another stile brings us into a small road where we pass the church and schoolhouse on our right and are shortly out at the main road.

We turn left for a few yards, and opposite the Crockham Hill post office and general stores which sells ices and confectionery, we turn right on another road thus doubling back for a short distance before we turn left on a signposted footpath to Limpsfield which starts as a small road containing some attractive houses. As the lane bears right and becomes unsurfaced we turn left over a stile by the side of a house and continue downhill with a hedge on our right. At the bottom of the slope we cross a barrier and turn right through a strip of woodland, go over a stream and stile and forward along a field with the hedge on our right. As the field ends we continue direction over a stile and across the centre of a wide field with the house called Trevereux over on our right, after passing which we bear right to a cottage just beyond the house. These field footpaths are not always visible on the ground and are decidedly muddy after wet winter weather.

We go through a gate near the cottage taking us into a lane where we turn right uphill, later passing springs in the fields on our right. Near the top of the hill, and immediately after the drive of a house called Graces, we turn right on a footpath and continue direction when we merge with a lane coming in on the left. We pass occasional houses on the right and at a drive we turn right for a short distance and just after the drive goes downhill we turn left uphill into trees coming out to a wide crossing track where we turn right. After a short distance we turn left on a tarmac drive going uphill through forestry plantations and when finally reaching the road we cross to a small footpath opposite.

We turn left, parallel with the road for a short distance and opposite a National Trust sign on the other side of the road we turn right on a small footpath taking us into a wooded area, mostly conifers. At a main and very straight crossing track we turn left, soon bearing right with the track and later at a fork going left downhill. We are soon at a crossing track with a water tank on our right and we take an opposite uphill path which soon merges with a path feeding in on the right and flattens out, giving good views of the North Downs ahead. We are now in the area known as The High Chart. We continue on this main path later bearing right and ignoring a left fork. At the next fork we take the smaller path on the left, continue over a crossing track, still with fine views on the left, and then go slightly downhill to a junction of paths. Here we go over a wide crossing track to a water tank and bear left slightly uphill. We soon have conifers on our right and hedgerow and open fields on our left and we continue for well over a quarter of a mile finally coming out to the road.

We cross to a gate opposite taking us into a Forestry Commission area known as Goodley Stock and bear left, keeping to the edge of the woods. When our path forks we keep left and when joined by a track coming in on the right we bear left with the path till it ends at a stile taking us into a wide track which we cross to another stile opposite.

Both walks now follow the same route
Once over the stile we go through a few trees to another stile, cross a field to two more stiles in quick succession and continue with a pavilion and sports field on our left, at the end of which we bear right downhill to yet another stile. We can enjoy fine views as we drop downhill to a lodge where a final stile brings us into a small drive on which we turn left with a small lake on our left and the river on our right. Just past a footbridge on our right we bear right on a path passing a beautiful cottage on our left and, going uphill to a stile, we are soon out to a small road. We cross to an enclosed footpath which finally turns left through the Kings Arms car park and brings us to a bus stop in the main road of Westerham opposite the George and Dragon.

Refreshment: Westerham where there are several inns and tea shops and at Crockham Hill.

Brasted

Scords Wood and Ide Hill
$6\frac{3}{4}$ miles

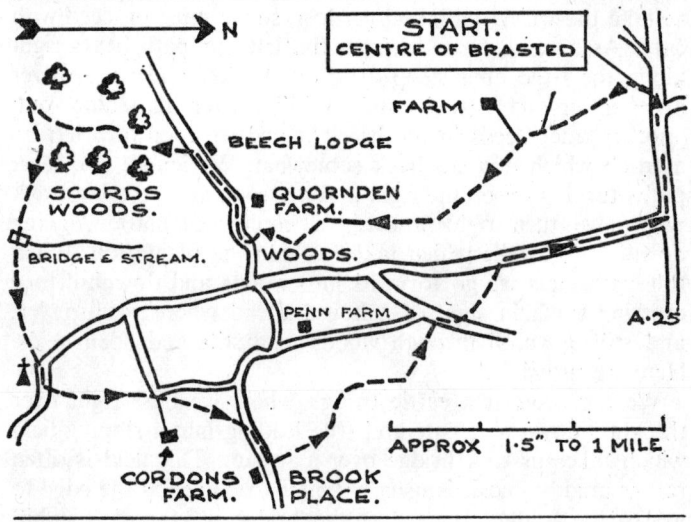

ALTHOUGH some mud must be expected in low-lying fields in winter this is a suitable walk for any time of year.

How to get there: By 483 bus (not Sundays), Green Line 705. By car on the A.25. Limited parking in the main street.

From the centre of Brasted near the pedestrian crossing we turn up Elliotts Lane passing some picturesque cottages after which the lane becomes a footpath. About half a mile further on we pass a few cottages on the right and when the track bears right into farm buildings we keep left on a bridleway with woods sloping up on our left. After another half a mile, at a junction of paths, we keep forward slightly uphill, finally crossing a stile into a field where we keep to the edge with Charman's Wood on our left. We go uphill and downhill to another stile and as we go forward along the edge of the

17

next field the buildings of Quornden Farm come into sight ahead on our right. After a third stile we turn sharply left uphill keeping close to the woods on our left and are soon out at the road where we turn right for a quarter of a mile.

Opposite the next house on the right, Beech Lodge, we turn left on a bridleway into woods, continuing over the first crossing track. We are now in Scords Wood, where it is quite easy to take the wrong path and get lost, so we must proceed with care. As a track feeds in from the left our path bears right along the edge of a steep drop on the left and we go over another crossing track and uphill. After flattening out, another track feeds in on the right and we soon turn left on a track which doubles back somewhat. We ignore two faint paths turning off on the right and are soon at a crossing track where we turn right towards a conifer plantation, going downhill to a stile which takes us into the plantation. When this path ends we go forward into woods and downhill to a crossing track in sight of a house ahead where we turn left and still downhill through woods to a stile and open fields. Here we turn left.

We are soon at a cattle trough where we bear right over the grass down to a gate and stile leading into a sloping field which takes us to a bridge over a stream. This field is often rather muddy and it is usually better to go round the edge to get to the bridge. Once over the bridge we turn left uphill towards Ide Hill church. Near the top at a bend in the track we turn right over a stile in the hedge and go forward on a small path round the side of Ide Hill, with a wire fence and fine views on our right and wooded slopes on our left. A stile takes us into woods and we soon cross two small streams and continue uphill through woods keeping to the main path. At a fork we keep left steeply uphill, emerging into a clearing on the top of Ide Hill.

From the clearing we make for the top of the hill among a few pine trees, passing the National Trust sign and keeping forward with a wire fence on the left. On reaching a drive to the vicarage we turn left and are soon out on the village green of Ide Hill. We cross the green to The Cock Inn which we pass as we continue down a minor road on the left

18

of the main road. This soon turns left and ends as a residential cul-de-sac with a green "island" opposite which is a signposted footpath to Brook Place. We go over the stile and cross a sloping field on a well defined footpath enjoying pleasant aspects. A squeeze stile brings us out on to a drive to Cordons Farm and without going out to the nearby road we turn right for a few yards and left at a brick gate post on a small path skirting the edge of a bungalow garden. An iron gate gives us access to a field and we keep forward with the fence on our right. As the field ends we turn right through a squeeze stile and maintain our original direction with a hedgerow and later a fence on our left, gradually going downhill to a gate and the road where we turn right.

We soon pass Brook Cottage and Brook Place with its stream fed by local springs. Opposite a barn we turn left on a track, passing on our right a row of brick houses and continuing forward with the stream over on our left among the trees. We maintain direction into the next field with an uphill slope on our right and after going under telegraph wires we bear left through a gate and slightly downhill into trees. We are soon at a wooden barrier where we turn left to a bridge over the stream after which we turn right on a slightly uphill path through trees, continuing direction when we emerge into an open field. After passing a yellow waymark on a post on our left we bear slightly left uphill towards some trees where we turn left over a stile. There is usually no footpath visible on the ground but after going forward and slightly right, aiming at the centre of the highest part of this sloping field, we come to a bar stile set in a wire fence.

Here we look back to admire the view and continue diagonally right over three more stiles, finally coming out to the road through two successive gates.

We turn right down the road for rather less than 100 yards to take a footpath on the left. When this forks almost at once we follow the right fork with a sweet chestnut plantation on our left and are soon out to another road where we turn right for just over half a mile. On reaching the main road A.25 we turn left for about a quarter of a mile to The White Hart and bus stop at Brasted.

Ide Hill

**Hanging Bank, Sheephill Wood, Wickhurst Manor. 6 miles
Hanging Bank, Sheephill Wood, Everlands. 5 miles**

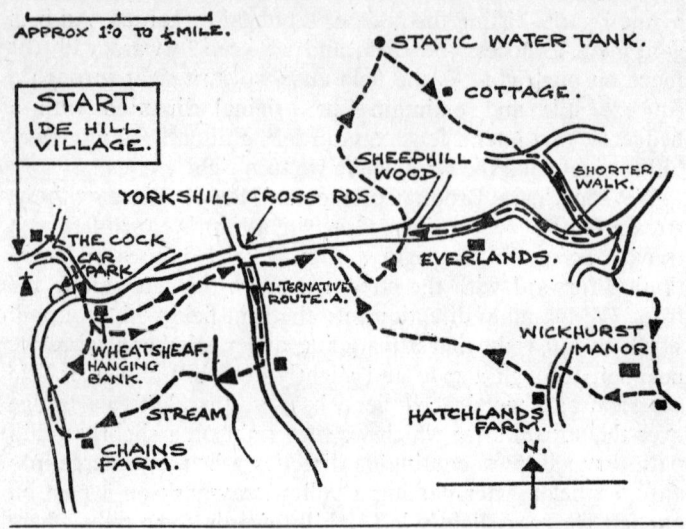

THOUGH there may be a little mud in winter this is a walk for any time of the year.

How to get there: By 404 (not Sundays) bus to Ide Hill. By car on the A.25 turning south at Sundridge for 3 miles.

Starting from the bus stop in Ide Hill village we continue past The Cock, bearing right on the Sevenoaks Road and soon passing on our right the village hall behind which is a small car park. We are now at a T junction and bear left towards The Wheatsheaf Inn, keeping it on our left as we go down a small side road, taking the left hand higher path leading us around the hillside known as Hanging Bank. We are soon at a junction of paths in a clearing and take the second path on our left, in a short distance at a fork keeping

20

right and continuing on through conifer plantations, ignoring side turnings. Later we go through an area of chestnuts with bluebells in late spring and, ignoring a small fork on the right, we go slightly uphill to a crossing track where we turn right. Our path continues on, still in woods, with a steep drop on our right, finally coming out to a small car park on our left at the Yorkshill cross roads.

Maintaining direction we cross Yorkshill Road and go through wooden posts to a very pleasant open area of pine trees. Ignoring a downhill path on the right we remain parallel with the road on our left and continue through open woods with some fine specimens of beech. Our path again touches the road on our left by a small car parking area but we continue forward over a log barrier on an uphill footpath which bears away from the road taking us into an area of spectacular beeches, abundant bluebells in season and fine views of Bough Beech reservoir on the right where the ground slopes precipitously down. Our path finally turns sharply left taking us back to the road which we cross to a footpath and stile opposite.

We now enter a conifer plantation, Sheephill Wood, on a small path which twists and turns till we cross another stile and turn left along a grassy track. Going over a drive to another stile we continue on a downhill path to a crossing track where we turn right uphill between plantations. At the top of the hill we ignore a turning on the left and keep forward, later passing a turning on the right and eventually coming out in a large clearing with a junction of paths and a static water tank.

We take the path immediately on our right, thus doubling back somewhat, soon ignoring a right fork. We can enjoy good views from this path and when it bears right we continue straight ahead on a small signposted footpath taking us downhill and out to a clearing. After crossing a stile we continue direction on a wide grassy track soon going over another stile at the side of a gate with a cottage in a clearing over on our left. Just past the house we take a signposted footpath on the left, immediately crossing a wide forestry track and continuing forward, slightly uphill. Eventually we emerge on a forestry track where we turn right, later bearing right and downhill to the road.

We turn left for a short distance then right on a minor road with pleasant aspects. Later the road goes uphill and we pass on our right the drive of Everlands.

For the shorter version

We go over the stile at the side of the Everlands drive, keeping right when our track forks. We soon have open aspects on our left and later, a sight of Bough Beech reservoir glistening in the distance. The house "Everlands" comes into sight down among the trees on our left and our path takes us through an area of rhododendrons before going downhill and out to a private drive where we turn left. We pass a footpath sign on a tree and go right at a fork, continuing slightly uphill past one or two cottages. We can enjoy fine views on our left before passing a lodge on our right and reaching the road where we turn left for a few yards before taking a signposted footpath on the left taking us into woods. When we reach the edge of an escarpment with fine views our path bears right and gradually takes us back close to the road again at a small car parking area which we cross, continuing direction. After going through a pleasant open area of pines we are out at the Yorkshill road.

For the longer version

About 80 yards beyond the Everlands drive we turn right down a drive to a red brick house and immediately turn left on an enclosed footpath taking us downhill to a lower road. We turn right for a few yards before taking another enclosed footpath on the left, by a $2\frac{1}{2}$ ton notice, going downhill past one or two pleasant houses. After coming out on a surfaced drive we continue downhill, go through a gate and bear left. Later after passing the second of two entrances to Wickhurst Manor we turn right on a surfaced track. We pass the front of the 15th century manor house and farm buildings and opposite a barn cross a stile on our left to take a signposted footpath, continuing direction round the edge of a field with a brick cottage on our right. Keeping the hedge on our right we turn left and right with the shape of the field, finally at a stile turning right uphill and coming out to the road where we turn left.

After a few yards we turn right over a stile with Hatchlands Farm on our left, bearing left to another stile taking us into a farm track where we turn right. The track ends with a stile and we then bear diagonally left over a field to a stile in trees ahead, crossing a ditch by an earth bridge and noticing the house, "Everlands", higher up the slope on our right. The stile takes us to a clear path through a small wood and on emerging we turn left uphill to go through a protected wire fence. We then bear diagonally right uphill going through the remains of a line of trees and over an uneven and hilly field to a stile at the side of a gate, after which we continue forward with woods on our right. As the field tapers to a corner we go over a stile and forward on an enclosed footpath with open fields on our left and tree covered slopes on our right. As our path gradually goes uphill we can see Bough Beech reservoir in the distance on our left and eventually we come out to the road by a small car parking area. We continue on, re-entering the woods and bearing slightly left. We are now retracing our steps over an earlier part of the walk and soon go through the area of pines and out to the Yorkshill road.

Both walks now follow the same route and we have two alternatives

(a) Along the top of the ridge for one mile.

(b) Downhill to Yorkshill Farm and over open hillside, a distance of two miles. This route includes a short but very steep uphill path.

(a) We cross the Yorkshill road, go through the small car parking space, continuing direction and later, when the path forks, going left. With a conifer plantation on our left we go over a diagonal crossing track, thus keeping straight ahead through pleasant woodland on a higher path than the one we used earlier in the walk. Later we have a wire fence and a drop on our left and our path bears right, soon joining a wider track at a lower level. We turn left on this lower track, thus doubling back for a short distance, and continue on downhill to a junction of paths with a patch of grass in the centre. We take the path on our right and retrace our steps back to the side of the Wheatsheaf Inn. We continue forward bearing right uphill for Ide Hill village, or bearing left for the small car park behind the village hall.

(b) We turn left down Yorkshill Road for about a third of a mile and opposite Yorkshill Farm buildings we turn right through a gate on a signposted footpath with a hedge and ditch on our right. After crossing a stream on an earth bridge we still keep the hedge on our right, going slightly uphill to a stile and continuing to a drive. Here we turn sharp left to cross a stile at the side of a garage, continuing forward over an uneven field with a hedge and a dip on our right. We soon bear slightly left keeping a small pond on our right and crossing a ditch, after which we continue with a hedge on our left. A stile takes us into the next field which we cross to another stile opposite. We cross the next hilly field diagonally left, enjoying good views of Bough Beech reservoir before we go over a gate and forward to picturesque Chains Farm, where we bear right up a drive.

On reaching the road we turn right uphill for 100 yards or so when we turn right on a signposted footpath taking us diagonally left over an uneven field, making for a stile visible against trees and just beyond a telegraph pole. We cross this stile, a ditch and two more stiles in quick succession then bear left uphill to yet another stile hidden in trees in the top left hand corner of the field. The last few yards before this stile are very steep but within the capacity of most able bodied people. Once over the stile we turn left in a drive, passing a few beautiful houses as we go uphill, and finally coming out to the road with the Wheatsheaf Inn on our right. We continue forward bearing right for Ide Hill village, or bearing left for the small car park behind the village hall.

Refreshment: Ide Hill.

Yorkshill

Bore Place, Bough Beech Reservoir. 6 miles
Field walk omitting Bore Place and the Reservoir. 4½ miles

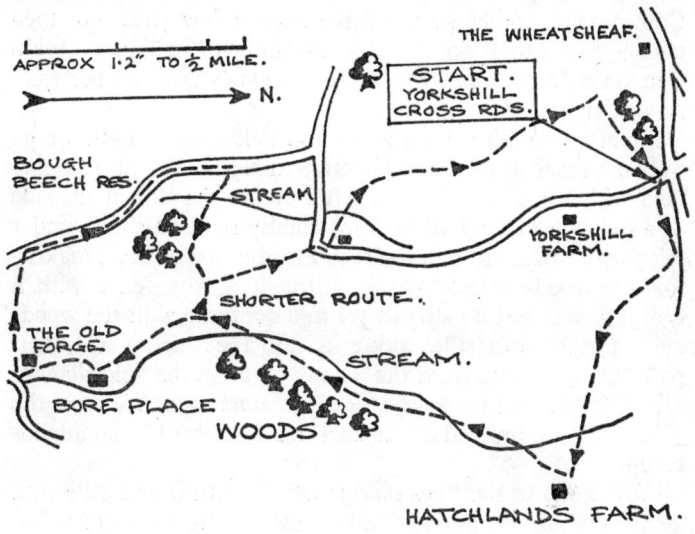

THIS is an interesting walk taking us downhill through pasture and farmland to the pleasantly landscaped Bough Beech Reservoir. In winter the low lying fields are bound to be muddy.

How to get there: 404 bus (not Sundays). By car to Ide Hill on the A.25 turning south at Sundridge for three miles.

This walk starts from a car parking space at the Yorks Hill crossroads where the bus stops and can easily be reached by turning eastwards out of Ide Hill village past the Wheatsheaf Inn on the B.2042 and taking the first right fork. The car parking space is on the right at the crossroads near a house called "Keepers" on the left, rather less than half a mile beyond the Wheatsheaf. There is another car parking space,

25

also on the right, about 300 yards further on.

From the car parking space we cross the minor road which goes downhill to Yorkshill Farm and take a footpath parallel with the road on our left. We go through posts and slightly uphill into a pleasant area of pines, and after a steep drop on our right our path bears left towards the road and another car parking space (the second mentioned above). Continuing parallel with the road for a few yards we then take a footpath forking right downhill—there is a footpath sign on a tree—later enjoying good views through the trees on our right.

Eventually with a wire fence and field on our right we go over a barrier to continue direction along the top of a sloping field with woods on our left. After crossing a stile at the side of a gate we go forward bearing slightly right downhill, under telegraph wires, through the remains of a line of trees, making for the woods ahead. We go through a wire fence with a footpath sign but no stile as yet and continue with the woods on our right to a stile taking us into the woods on a clear path. On emerging from the woods we cross the field diagonally right making for a stile visible against trees. We cross the stile and continue along a cart track towards Hatchlands Farm.

At the end of the trees on our left we turn over a stile with farm buildings on our left* and after leaving the farm buildings we bear right to the end of some woods on the left. We continue direction to cross a small stream between the woods on the left and a row of trees on the right and go forward with the stream and a wire fence on our left. At the end of the field we go through a removable wire barrier and turn left on a track going slightly uphill along the edge of a field with woods on our left. We are soon at a metal gate leading into woods but we take a stile on the right taking us into the field where we continue with the wire fence, ditch and woods on our left. There are very pleasant aspects to enjoy and after well over a quarter of a mile we bear right with the line of the woods, soon bearing left through a gate into the next

---

* This footpath will shortly be diverted through the farm buildings.

field. The footpath is down the centre of this long narrow field but in practice it will be found easier to keep to the edge with the woods on our right. At the end of the field we go through a gap in the hedge and bear right round the edge of the next field with the hedgerow on our right. Opposite a telegraph pole on the left we bear right over a stream into a wide track.

For the shorter version
We turn right at this track and follow it for half a mile until it comes to a small road.

For the longer version
We turn left along the wide track, pass a house on the left and continue on through farm buildings, passing on our left Bore Place dating back to the 15th century or even earlier. After about a quarter of a mile along the drive we come out to the road and take a stile on the right at the side of the garden gate of The Old Forge, a picturesque house built in 1745. We go over a foot-bridge and up the field with the garden hedge on our right and crossing a stile continue direction with a wire fence on our right. When this ends we continue forward going slightly uphill, passing on our left one or two free standing trees in a small hollow. We are soon going slightly downhill and make for a stile in the bottom right hand corner of the field. This brings us to the road where we turn right and are soon passing the Bough Beech Reservoir, the borders of which have been made into a nature reserve.

We leave the water behind and continue up the road passing one or two pleasant houses on the right. Soon after the last house we turn right through a gate on a signposted foot-path and go forward with the hedge on our right to cross a small stream in a belt of trees. We continue direction up a sloping field with pleasant aspects all round and a good view of the reservoir on our right, making for a gap in the trees ahead. Once inside the wood we turn left on a clear wide track enclosed in a narrow strip of wood. After about a quarter of a mile we come out through a gate from where we can see the spire of Ide Hill church visible on the skyline ahead.

Both versions now follow the same route

We go forward to the road where we turn right for a few yards then left on a signposted footpath with a couple of red brick cottages on our right. We go over a barrier and down a slightly sloping field with the hedge on our left, soon going over a gate on our left and continuing direction with the hedgerow on our right. Before long another stile on our right takes us into a strip of woods, over a stream on a footbridge and out to another field. We go forward and slightly uphill to two gates in the top right hand corner of the field, if cropped keeping to the edge with the hedge on the right. Once through the left hand gate we bear right with the hedge on our right going along the edge of a narrow field and turning left for a few yards at the end to go over a double wire fence, partially protected but lacking a proper stile. We go forward over the centre of a field to a gap in the trees and a path through a strip of woods, emerging in an open field sloping slightly uphill. The line of the footpath is diagonally left over the field but if crops are growing, usually maize, it is easier to bear left round the edge. At the top left hand corner of the fields we go over a stile and continue up the next field with woods on our left and Yorkshill Farm visible on our right. We turn left over a stile at the corner of the field and forward for a few yards to a drive where we turn right uphill passing a house on the left.

As the drive bears left we turn sharply right into trees on a track which soon bears left uphill to a narrow crossing track where we turn right. Further along this path we can enjoy beautiful views on our right before we bear left uphill, finally bearing right to the car parking space at the Yorkshill crossroads.

Sundridge

**Dryhill Picnic Park, Mill Bank Woods, Greenlane Woods
8 miles
Dryhill Picnic Park, Greenlane Woods. 5 miles**

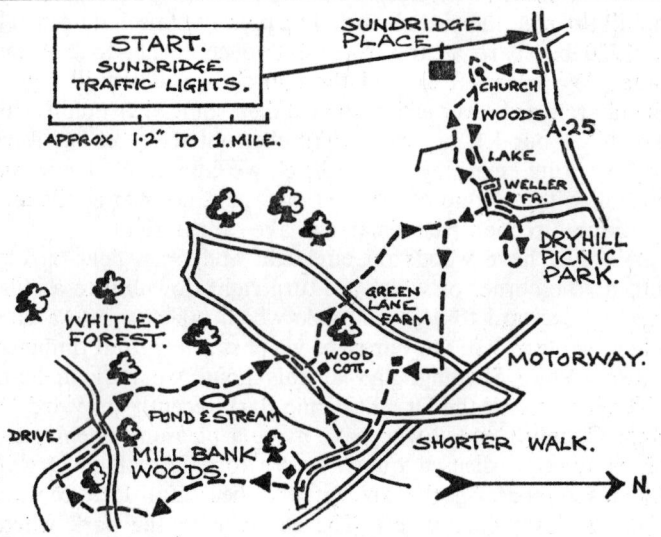

THIS walk gives plenty of variety: field walking with wide views, pleasant open woodland, springs and streams and the sight of some delightful old period houses. Dryhill Picnic Park is a splendid amenity for families offering scope for "exploration" and providing good views. A walk suitable for any time of the year but with some mud in winter. One of the farms passed on this walk has a herd of magnificent highland cattle.

How to get there: 483 bus (not Sundays) or Green Line 705 to Sundbridge. Car parking facilities at Sundridge are practically non-existent and motorists would be advised to continue past the traffic lights at Sundridge and in just under a mile turning right by some nurseries up Dryhill Lane to the Dryhill Picnic Park where there is ample parking. Starting at Dryhill shortens the walk by 2¼ miles.

Leaving the bus stop at the Sundridge traffic lights we continue along the main road A.25 towards Sevenoaks for about 100 yards, when we turn right on a signposted footpath taking us past a field with caravans on our left. We cross a stile and make for the church, keeping along the edge of the field and uphill through the churchyard. The present church dates back to 1220 but parts of the tower date even earlier to Norman times. We bear left around the church and downhill out of the churchyard, over a tiny stream then somewhat uphill with woods on our left, a few ancient chestnut trees on our right and a spring emerging from a brick wellhouse. We later pass a knoll with a group of trees on our right, go over a stile and continue direction past a narrow lake on the right.

We now have woods on our right and open field on our left, at the corner of which we turn right downhill to a stile, keeping forward to a second stile which takes us into a lane where we turn left. On our right we pass a beautiful timbered house, White Sheiling, and at this point we may make a diversion to visit the Dryhill Picnic Park recently provided by Kent County Council who have made a pleasant amenity out of an area of disused quarries. We turn left along Dryhill Lane soon passing the ancient and beautiful 15th century Wellers Farm on our left. The entrance to the park where there are toilets is on the right, a short distance past the farm, and a tarmac drive takes us forward past high cliffs on our left. When the drive ends we continue direction on a wide grassy ride soon with another crag on our right and later with a small embankment on our left and fine open aspects on the right. The grassy ride bears right, circling round the park area and returning us finally to the end of the tarmac drive.

From Dryhill Picnic Park we turn left in Dryhill Lane, continuing past the front of White Sheiling and ignoring the lane on the right. We go slightly uphill and pass the ruins of Dryhill on the left and an exquisite timbered house on the right. At a bend in the lane we turn left through a gate on a

30

signposted bridleway, keeping along the edge of the field with the hedge on our left and later going through another gate still maintaining direction. We now have the hedge on our right and pleasant aspects on the left with Polhill in the distance. Continuing with a wire fence on the left and woods on the right we finally go downhill and out to a small road. Crossing to a signposted footpath opposite we go uphill through a fringe of trees, over a stile and turn right on a crossing track. Our track later goes slightly uphill, passes some barns on the right and turns left, finally bringing us out to a road which we cross to a smaller road opposite. This twists steeply downhill.

For the shorter version

When the road flattens out at the bottom of the hill we turn right over a stile on a signposted footpath and go uphill a short distance to cross another stile on the right. With a wire fence on our left we continue uphill for about a quarter of a mile enjoying pleasant views and finally turning right and over a stile to the road. We turn left and continue along the grass verge for about 200 yards when we cross to a cottage on the right and take a signposted footpath passing in front of the cottage (there is another one at the side of the cottage) passing on our left the remains of the old road.

For the longer version

We continue along the road and are within sight of the motorway when, just after passing a small turning on the right, we cross a stile on the right to a footpath, enclosed at first, taking us into a plantation. We stay on this path through Mill Bank Wood for nearly a mile, most of it in a small valley, until we go slightly uphill to a stile, bringing us to a road. Crossing to another stile opposite we continue forward on a track with a static water tank on our left, later being joined by a track coming in on the right before we bear left through trees and out to another road. We turn right up this minor road, enjoying pleasant aspects, and after about a quarter of a mile at a T junction we turn left for a short distance. Just before a private drive on the left we turn right over a stile to a grassy track, uphill at first. We ignore a sign-posted footpath on the left and go downhill with plantations on either side later bearing left and ignoring what might seem like a continuation of our path straight ahead. We are still going downhill when we turn sharply right on a small signposted footpath taking us into trees. After a few yards we go over a stile and bear right for a few yards then forward with a line of trees on our left, fairly soon turning through the trees and continuing down the field with the trees on our right. Passing under the telegraph wires we go forward a few yards then bear left downhill to the bottom of a small valley.

Here we turn right on a track soon passing on our right a spring emerging from the embankment and forming a small stream and we continue forward through a gate with a stile soon passing a ruined wall on our left and the dried up mill pond and ruins of Whitley Mill on our right, claimed to be the site of a phantom horseman. For a while our track follows the line of the telegraph wires then becomes raised with a drop on either side and finally goes uphill to a stile and a road where we turn right.

After a short distance the road bears right while we bear left on to the old road towards a cottage, turning left in front of the cottage on a signposted footpath.

Both walks now follow the same route

We go over a stile at the side of a gate and continue on a footpath enclosed at first, later through Greenlane Wood, and downhill through an O-shaped stile. We now have woods on our right, a young plantation on our left and pleasant aspects ahead. After crossing a wire barrier we pass a house in a dip on our right and finally come out to the road where we turn left for a few yards then right on a signposted footpath taking us uphill. Passing woods on our left we take a stile on our left near the corner of the field, cross a track to another stile then bear right keeping to the edge of the field with the hedgerow on our right. We go slightly downhill to the end of the field then bear right on an enclosed track which we follow for about half a mile, later bearing left and downhill past the Dryhill ruins which we passed earlier in the walk. If we are returning to the Picnic Park we keep straight ahead but if returning to Sundridge for the bus we turn left at the side of White Sheiling but ignore the stile on our right and as our track bears left around a bungalow we maintain direction on a small enclosed footpath.

Later our path bears right, still between hedges, and from this point as an alternative it is possible to use a cart track on the left hand side of the footpath, with open fields on the left. Continuing direction, we go over a very wide crossing track after which our track is enclosed with a wire fence on the right and a hedge on the left. Later Sundridge Place Farm comes into sight ahead and we turn right over a stile, going diagonally left across the field towards Sundridge Church. We go over another stile and downhill bearing left over the little stream before going uphill to the churchyard. After bearing right around the church we leave the churchyard and keep along the left hand side of the field to the stile ahead. A short distance along an enclosed footpath brings us out to the main road which we cross turning left alongside a tributary of the River Darent and are soon at the traffic lights and bus stop at Sundridge.

Refreshment: An inn at Sundridge.

Dunton Green
Otford 4½ miles or 6 miles

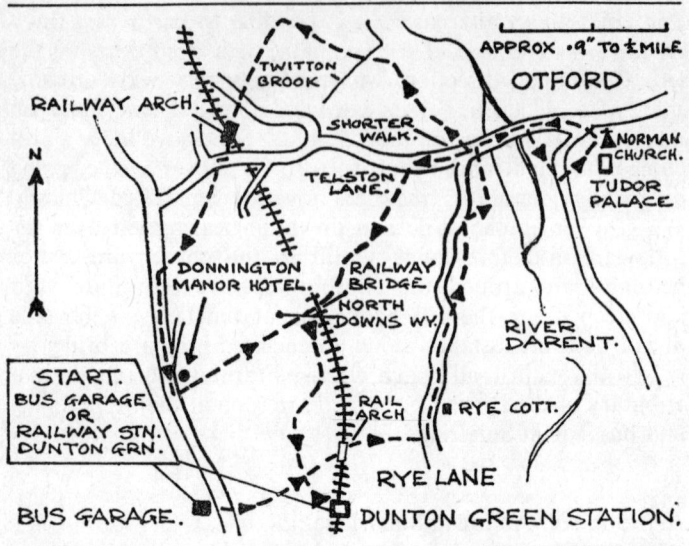

THIS is mainly a field walk and is recommended for summer. The chief interest centres around the historic buildings to be seen in Otford, above all, the remains of the Tudor Palace in its pleasant and homely setting. Apart from one or two gentle slopes the walk is on level ground.

How to get there: By train to Dunton Green Station where there is a car park. Green Line 704 and buses 402, 404, 413, 421, 431/431A, 454/454A, 471.

From the bus garage at Dunton Green we cross the road on the pedestrian crossing and go forward on a signposted tarmac footpath leading across a field to a lamp-post. From the railway station we go down steps opposite the station buildings, under a subway and forward over a field on a tarmac footpath to the lamp-post where we turn sharp right over the field towards the railway line. Coming from the bus station we continue similarly from the lamp-post. We are soon at a stile, go under a railway arch, over another stile and keep forward across a wide field gradually getting nearer the wire fence on our left. The path is not visible on the ground.

A bar stile eventually brings us out into Rye Lane where we turn left soon passing Rye Cottage on our right. We continue along this quiet lane for half a mile enjoying views on the right. When the road bears sharply left, to avoid the bend, we continue forward on a signposted footpath with a house and garden on the left. (If the footpath is overgrown the road may be used instead.) Our footpath touches the road later and continues over a stile taking us across the drive and front garden of a house, The Firs, and to another stile bringing us into a field. We go forward across the field enjoying a good view of the Old Tudor Palace and Otford Mount over on our right, continuing on and through the next field and finally coming out to the road where we turn right. After a few yards we turn right again on a road taking us into a small housing estate, turn right into The Charne, and bear left at the central green, soon bearing left again on a concrete path. When we leave the houses behind we have an area of poplars on our right and on reaching the main road through Otford we turn right.

We keep to this road for rather less than a quarter of a mile, crossing a tributary and the River Darent and passing on our right some fine old houses, including Broughton Manor basically Tudor with 18th century additions, and Pickmoss, a picturesque timbered house built in the 14th and 15th centuries. At a butchers shop on a corner we turn right down Pickmoss Lane, continuing on an enclosed footpath and after a kissing gate maintaining direction along the side of a field. Another kissing gate brings us to the road which we cross diagonally left to the entrance to Palace Fields. We continue on a surfaced footpath over the grass, later bearing right towards the ruined remains of a splendid Tudor Palace. In the early 16th century it originally belonged to the Archbishop of Canterbury and it later passed to Henry VIII who once stayed there with a retinue of 4,000. Curiously part of the remains of the palace buildings have been embodied in a row of cottages which stand between a tower and part of the main gatehouse, turned into a dovecot in the 19th century. There is a stream at the rear of the ruins and though not far from the main road it makes a pleasant picnic spot.

Leaving Palace Fields we pass in front of the tower and bear left with a pleasant grass area on our left and on our right one or two beautiful ancient houses and the church with its low square Norman tower. We cross the road, keeping on our right the village pond, now isolated on an island amid traffic, and bear left down the road signposted to Bromley. We pass one or two inns, small shops and occasional picturesque houses and continue along the road.

For the shorter version

We walk along the road for about half a mile finally turning left down Telston Lane. We continue through this residential area for rather more than a quarter of a mile, passing on our right a general store for confectionery and ice cream, and later turning right then left through New Barn Farm after which our track goes uphill with orchards on our right. After crossing a railway bridge we turn left.

For the longer version

We walk along the road for about a quarter of a mile and opposite Rye Lane we turn right over a stile and cross a field keeping the electricity wires on our right. Another stile brings us to the corner of the next field and we continue with the hedge on our right for about a quarter of a mile, enjoying a pleasant view. We finally bear left for a few yards, over a stile and go slightly left then forward on a track taking us to a metal gate with a stile on the right giving access to a concrete bridge over Twitton Brook, a tributary of the Darent. We cross the brook and continue direction over a field to trees ahead, going between wooden posts in a corner of the field and forward through a gate and stile to a rutted lane enclosed in hedges. At a break in the hedge on our right where a path turns off at the side of a hopfield, we turn left over a bar stile and continue straight across a wide field making for a white house visible ahead. A stile brings us out to a road which we cross to a footpath opposite with the house on our right and soon we have a hedge on our left and open field on our right.

When the hedge ends we continue forward towards the railway on a field track, go under the railway arch and turn left on a track which soon takes us to the road. (The footpath line is actually a continuation of our original direction but because of growing crops the track bearing left is mostly used.) We cross the road to the field opposite and immediately turn right on a track at the side of the field, parallel with the road. Just after going under electricity wires we turn left over the field on a clear wide track which we follow for more than a third of a mile, gradually drawing nearer an embankment over on our right. We finally come out on the verge of a main road and turn left for Dunton Green, after about a quarter of a mile turning left at Donnington Manor.

Once through the hotel car park a footpath brings us to a stile and we go forward with the hedge on our right, continuing over another stile and up a sloping field. We are now on part of the North Downs Way, with a view across the hills which form part of the west side of the Darent Valley. A gentle uphill gradient takes us over a stile and a crossing track, under electricity wires and forward on a clear path through crop fields sloping downhill to a railway bridge where we turn right.

Both walks now follow the same route

We continue along the path with a wire fence on our left, later going through a strip of woods and bearing right over a field on a well defined path. We pass a clump of conifers on our left, go over a stile in the hedge at the corner of the field and continue downhill with the hedge on our right. At the bottom corner of the field we go over a stile and continue forward on a footpath taking us into the drive to Broughton House, after a few yards turning left on a path into woods. We soon emerge through a kissing gate and continue direction on a surfaced path over a field. On arriving at the lamp-post we turn left for the station and right for the bus garage.

Refreshment: Several inns at Otford and Dunton Green.

Otford

Shoreham, Polhill. 6 miles
Shoreham. 5¼ miles

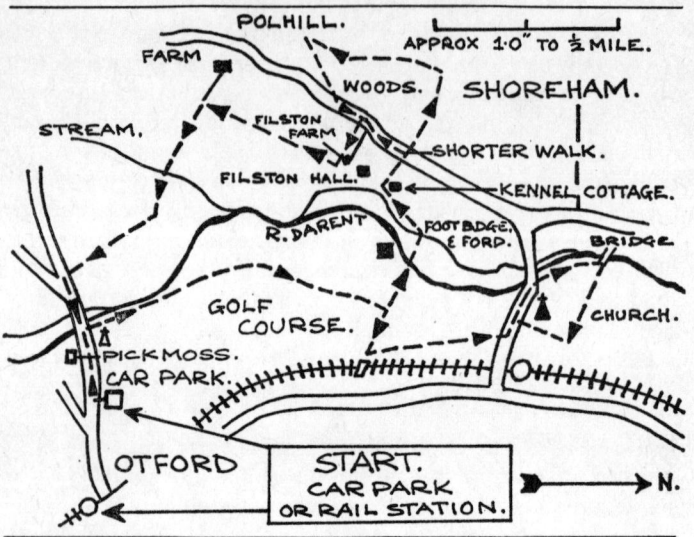

THE longer version of this walk is recommended. This is an enjoyable walk at any time of the year and not unduly muddy.
How to get there: By train to Otford Station. Buses 401 (also on Sundays), 404, 421, 421A (not Sundays). By car on the A.21 or A.225. There is a free car park and toilets opposite the school which is next door to The Bull Inn on the minor road through Otford.

The walk starts from the car park but if we are coming from the station we go down the station approach turning left at the main road and passing the village pond on a traffic island on our left. After about a quarter of a mile we reach the car park opposite the school.

built in the 14th to 15th centuries, we turn right on a sign-
our left the ancient timbered house, Pickmoss, which was
Leaving the car park we turn right and after passing on

38

posted footpath with the River Darent on our left. We pass several charming houses and the Old Mill and continue forward on a footpath over a stile and along the edge of a crop field, still with the river on our left. After passing under telegraph wires as the field ends we turn right for a few yards then left again on a well defined rising path taking us over the centre of a field.

We continue direction over a crossing track and now have a hedge on the right and pleasant wide views of the Darent Valley on our left. After a stile we continue through two more fields with a golf course on the left and hedge on the right, finally passing a few beech trees on the left and coming out on a stony track where we turn right. After about 100 yards we turn left passing a wooden building on our left and continuing forward on a wide track which later slopes downhill slightly and finally brings us on an enclosed footpath out to the road.

We turn left down the road and are soon in the picturesque village of Shoreham. Before reaching the bridge over the River Darent we may care to visit the church by turning right up the rising churchyard path opposite the Olde George Inn.

At the river bridge we should turn right keeping the river on our left but a short diversion across the bridge will enable us to see more of Shoreham. There is a post office and general stores on the right and a restaurant a short distance further on.

Returning over the bridge we turn left passing on our right several houses of character including Water House. We continue direction on a drive which soon becomes a footpath from which we can enjoy a view of fields, houses and cottage gardens across the river on our left. Our path ends at a bridge on our left but we turn right on an enclosed footpath soon turning right over a stile to a well defined field footpath. This takes us over a small tributary and after two more stiles we continue on an enclosed footpath taking us slightly uphill and finally over another stile to a crossing track. Here we turn right over a concrete stile keeping along the edge of a field with the hedgerow on our left. After another stile we continue direction on a track with the churchyard wall on our right. We are soon out in the road where we turn left. We are now retracing an earlier part of the walk but in reverse the views are different. We soon turn right on the enclosed footpath which later becomes a wider track and after about half a mile we are out on the stony track where we turn right continuing on downhill till we pause to admire on our left The Old Mill with its beautiful garden and mill pond.

Continuing on, our track soon brings us to a ford and a footbridge over a tributary of the Darent. We cross the bridge and turn left along the stream with open fields on our right. Later our path takes us between the stream and Kennel Cottage, an historic building of Kent, and we bear right around this beautiful house and garden and up a lane to the road.

For the shorter version omitting Polhill
At the road we turn left walking along the verge for about 200 yards and turn left again on a footpath signposted to Twitton parallel with the Filston Farm track.

For the longer version up Polhill
At the road we cross to a signposted foopath taking us uphill continuing direction over a stile and on reaching a gate on the right leading into Meenfield Wood (Forestry Commission) we turn left on a small footpath over a field. We are soon at a concrete stile and continue forward on a well defined path which keeps to the edge of the woods, sloping slightly downhill. We join a wider track coming in on the right and maintain direction to a fork where we take the right hand rising path which soon narrows. Our path bears right and later at another fork we bear right up a small embankment coming out on to heathland on the side of Polhill.

We turn right, going steeply uphill with trees on our right and a more open area with young beeches on our left. After about 50 yards just before our path goes into trees we bear left on a small path. We soon bear right uphill and immediately left again and continue on a more level path with woods on our right. We finally join a wider track which would take us to the top of Polhill if we turned right but if we want a pleasant spot for a rest or a picnic there are plenty of suitable places only a little further up the hillside. From here we can enjoy magnificent views of the Darent Valley spread out before us and in summer we can see many varieties of wild flowers of the chalk downland on this stretch of heathland.

To continue our walk we turn left downhill, thus doubling back at a lower level, soon going through posts and diagonally downhill on a clear path through cropfields. A stile brings us to the road where we turn left, soon turning right on a signposted footpath to Twitton parallel with the Filston Farm track.

Both walks now follow the same route

We soon bear right following round the farm buildings and turn right on a wide track taking us across crop fields where we can enjoy pleasant views on both sides. Our track bends slightly to the left and continues its original direction with a hedgerow and later a hop field on the left. We finally come to a crossing track where we turn left between hedges on a rutted lane. We soon go over a stile at the side of a gate and forward across a field to a bridge over a stream and another stile. Our track soon bears left and we go over a stile on the right and bear left round the edge of a field with the hedgerow on our left. As the hedge ends we go over a stile and continue direction over a field to a gate and stile bringing us out to the road where we turn left for about a quarter of a mile to the car park opposite the school at Otford.

Refreshment: Otford and Shoreham where there is a choice of inn and a restaurant.

Eynsford

Lullingstone, Shoreham. 6 miles
Lullingstone. $3\frac{1}{2}$ miles

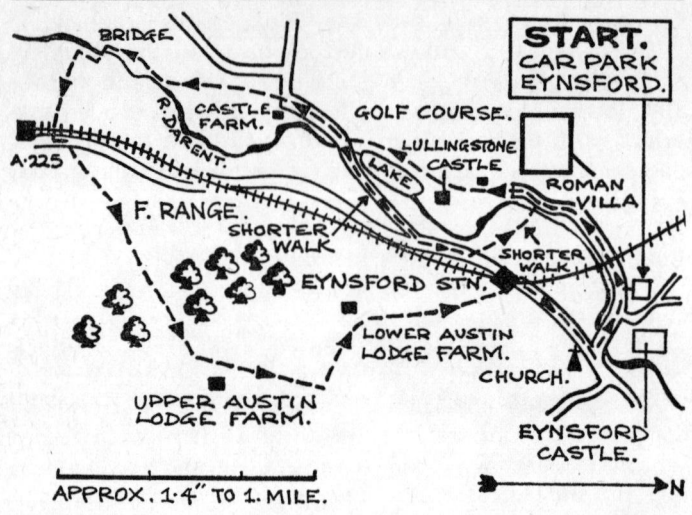

APPROX. 1·4" TO 1 MILE.

IN this walk we explore further up the Darent valley enjoying river scenery and venturing into the hills and little valleys on the east side. Those with a taste for history will find plenty of interest in the Roman Villa and the remains of Eynsford THE beginning and end of this walk are on hard surfaced roads or lanes but the countryside in the middle more than compensates for this.

How to get there: By 404 bus. By train to Eynsford Station. By car on the A.225 and there is a free car park next to The Plough Inn.

This walk starts from the free park in Eynsford next door to The Plough. If starting from the railway station turn to the end of the walk which passes the station on the return.

We begin with an optional half mile diversion to visit the

remains of Eynsford Castle, dating from the early 12th century. For this visit we turn left over the 17th century bridge and left again on the A.225 opposite the church, passing several of Eynsford's most picturesque houses and one or two shops. There is a particularly pleasing cluster of wooden fronted cottages on the right near the war memorial. Opposite the Castle Hotel we turn left for the entrance to the ruins of Eynsford Castle.

We retrace our steps through Eynsford, turning right over the bridge, continuing past the Plough on the grass verge at the riverside and later maintaining direction up a lane passing an ancient and beautiful cottage on our right. Ignoring a right turning we make for the railway viaduct ahead, with the river and meadows on our left providing pleasant views. After another quarter of a mile or so we reach the Lullingstone Roman Villa which dates back to 80–90 A.D. and is most attractively presented by the Department of the Environment.

With the Roman Villa on our right we continue direction taking a private road with the river on the left and one or two houses on the right. Just after a quarter of a mile we pass on our left Lullingstone Castle with its brick Tudor gateway and the main building behind, misleadingly called a castle and looking more like an 18th century residence, though it is actually much older. Up to the 18th century there was a second gatehouse behind the one we see and the house was moated.

Just past the gatehouse the track bears right to a golf course but we continue direction on a small footpath with a lake and later, the river on our left. This path is not a public right of way but the public are permitted to use it by courtesy of the landowner. After a quarter of a mile or so we come out to a small road.

For the shorter version
We turn left for half a mile and left again on reaching the A.225. We now have to endure the main road for a quarter of a mile and can remain on the left hand side walking along the verge, or, if we prefer it, cross over to the other side and

scramble up a small embankment to a much pleasanter path under trees, following the line of the road at a higher level. (If the embankment seems too steep we can turn right for about 30 yards to a point where it is lower.) After a quarter of a mile the path on the embankment drops down to road level and we cross to a footpath opposite, going first through a strip of woods and then with fields on either side. We finally go through farm buildings, cross the River Darent on a bridge and are soon at the Roman Villa, where we bear right on the lane along which we came earlier. We continue forward, going under the railway viaduct and bearing right into Eynsford finally reaching the car park at the side of the Plough.

If we are returning to Eynsford Station, after the embankment path drops down to road level we maintain direction on the old road, now a lay-by, bear right under the railway bridge and right again up the station approach road.

For the longer version

At the small road we continue direction, passing Castle Farm on our left and when the road turns right we continue forward on a grassy track with hop fields and cultivations either side. At a belt of poplars we maintain direction over a stile, go through a crop field, usually maize, and cross a concrete drive to two stiles in quick succession. We make for a stile in a wire fence visible ahead and continue to yet another stile going forward along a river-side path. The river is not always visible when the trees are in full leaf and at first it meanders some distance away from our path. We go over a stile and continue by the fence, pass through a gate to another stile by a brick footbridge and along an enclosed path coming out to the road where we turn left for a few yards, right on a path at the side of the mill house and left over a wooden footbridge over the river. After going forward for a few yards on an enclosed footpath we cross a stile and then immediately turn right along a slightly raised footpath over the meadow, soon going over two stiles to an enclosed footpath. We finally come out over a stile, cross a track to another stile with a metal gate on the right and continue direction up a field with the hedge on our right. After crossing the railway line our foopath soon brings us out to the main road, the A.225, where we turn left.

Ignoring a drive on the right, after about 40 yards we turn right on a signposted footpath going up a slight embankment then diagonally left on a well defined path over a maize field. On the far side of the field our path enters a wooded area on a gentle uphill gradient, bringing us out to the open where it bears right uphill. We continue across a stony drive enjoying fine views on our left and we re-enter a rather more wooded area bearing left uphill, and soon going up steeply under trees. At the top of the hill we are in a clearing with a flagpole indicating the firing range to the left. We go forward to a stile ahead taking us into a field and keep along the edge of the field with the fence on our left to another stile at the corner of the field, after which we go under a bar and continue direction into woods on a well defined path.

When we emerge from the woods we are joined by a path coming up on the left and we go forward bearing slightly right to a stone stile taking us into a field which we cross diagonally right. At the other side of the field we drop down to a stone stile taking us into woods. We go steeply downhill and are soon out on the open hillside above a beautiful valley. We continue downhill and the path soon bears left along the contour to a stile which we cross, turning right downhill with a hedge on the left. At the valley bottom we turn left along the edge of a crop field on a well defined track leading to Upper Austin Lodge Farm. Leaving the farm buildings to our right we then join the farm road, turning left along it for about one and a quarter miles enjoying pleasing aspects before passing Lower Austin Lodge Farm on the left and finally reaching Eynsford Station. Continuing past the station we are soon at the main road, the A.225 where we turn right downhill through a residential area for about a third of a mile. At the Eynsford church on our right we turn left, going over the bridge and past the Plough to the car park.

Refreshment: Inns at Eynsford and a cafe near the bridge.

Shoreham

Romney Street, Kemsing. 7 miles
Romney Street to Hillside above Kemsing. $5\frac{3}{4}$ miles

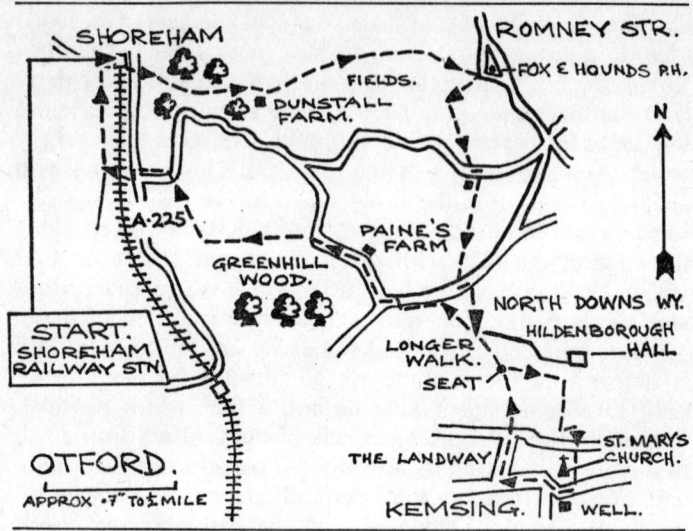

RECOMMENDED for a crisp autumn or spring day, but after wet weather the chalky slopes will be dangerously slippery.

How to get there: By train or 404 bus to Shoreham Station where there is a car park.

From the station approach at Shoreham Station we cross the road diagonally right to a signposted footpath and go uphill on an enclosed track, soon going through posts and taking the left one of two footpaths. We are soon in woods, presently going steeply uphill and when the path forks we may take either: the right hand one is a little wider but they are both as steep and join higher up at a crossing track. Continuing direction over this track we are soon over a stile and after a little more footpath, out into an open field.

On a path just visible on the ground we cross to farm

buildings ahead, going between outbuildings of Dunstall Farm and turning left on the wide gravel farm track. After a few yards we turn right on a cart track passing a barn on our left and going downhill then uphill with crop fields on our right. As the path flattens we bear left through a gate at the side of a broken down stile and cross a crop field on a well defined path, enjoying pleasant aspects and continuing across the next field. A stile takes us into woods on a downhill footpath which finally bears left and steeply down to another stile taking us out on to open hillside. We now bear diagonally left downhill on a faintly discernible footpath, enjoying pleasant views. We cross the bottom of the valley and go a little way up the other side to the corner of a wire fence on our right where we go over a stile under some trees and continue our original direction uphill with a hedge and later a fence on our left. We go over a stile at the top of the hill, forward over a crop field on a well defined path, pass the end of a hedgerow on our right and diagonally right uphill with a clump of trees on our right. As our path flattens out we continue across a stile and just past a house on our left we go over another stile to an enclosed footpath, shortly coming out at the Fox and Hounds, Romney Street.

Immediately opposite the public house we turn right over a stile and cross the field diagonally right on a faint path to another stile in the hedgerow. We cross the stile and turn left on an enclosed footpath soon going over bars and bearing left with the hedge on our left. As the field ends we go over a stile at the side of a telegraph pole and continue with fenced conifers on our right. Another stile takes us into an enclosed footpath and with a house on our right we go downhill and out to the road.

We turn left up the road for a few yards then right over a stile and cross the field slightly to the right, keeping some trees around a sunken pond on our left. Continuing forward, we later go through a gap in the trees ahead and emerge on to a hillside with a fine view across the valley. Bearing slightly left we go down to the valley bottom where we turn left and, as we approach the end of the valley, we soon turn right to a bar stile and a gentle rising enclosed footpath with conifer plantations either side. After about a quarter of a mile we are out on a small road where we turn left for a few yards then right on a surfaced drive, later turning left through the wicket gate to Hildenborough Hall. In a few yards we turn right on a signposted footpath and go forward along the edge of a field with the hedgerow on our right, turning left at the corner and ignoring various small paths turning off into the woods. As the field ends we bear right downhill through a strip of woods and out to the open hillside above Kemsing near a seat from which we can admire the view.

For the longer version

A few yards downhill from the seat we turn left on a small but well defined path which twists and turns along the hillside affording fine views and, in summer, taking us among a variety of wild flowers. We continue on over a stile and later when our path joins a track coming down on the left we continue on this wider track at first under trees and then out on to the open hillside again. With a seat up on our left we continue downhill over grass on a barely visible path to a fenced strip of trees where we turn left for about 30 yards to a stile which we cross dropping down into the road. We turn left for a few yards then right on a path leading into a recreation ground, going forward and slightly downhill with trees on our right. In the corner of the ground we turn right through a gate with the church on our right.

From the church we go forward down Church Lane turning right down the High Street and passing numerous beautiful and ancient houses, a shop or two, St. Edith Hall, built in 1911, two public houses and St. Edith's Well. Ignoring a road turning off on the left at the well we maintain direction past a few shops, turning right up The Landway, a residential road sloping gradually uphill to the main road.

We cross the road to a signposted footpath opposite and cross a crop field on a clear path. As the field ends we continue uphill on a path through a belt of trees soon coming out on to more open hillside and later passing the seat overlooking Kemsing.

Both walks now follow the same route

We will be retracing an earlier part of the walk for the next quarter of a mile and go steeply uphill through trees coming out to the open field where we turn left, following round two sides with trees on our left. We finally come out to the Hildenborough Hall drive and bear left to the wicket gate. We go over a stile opposite the gate on a signposted footpath which is part of the North Downs Way and cross the field diagonally right aiming at the corner of some woods ahead. Passing the corner of these woods on our left we continue direction along a narrow extension of the field to a stile in the corner taking us to the road.

We turn left and are soon at a road junction where we turn right on the road signposted to Shoreham. After about half a mile we turn left over a stile on a signposted footpath, going forward on a rough track which soon takes us into woods. We remain close to the edge of the woods with fields visible on our right and are later out on the open hillside with fine views on our left of Otford, Dunton Green and Chipstead Water in the far distance. We continue our direction and our path soon re-enters woods, goes slightly downhill and emerges again on an open hillside where we turn right enjoying fine views on our left. Once more our path enters woods and we fork left steeply downhill soon coming out into the open and continuing round the hillside. Our path gradually drops in height and finally at a fork we bear left downhill and out to the road.

We turn right for a few yards then left into an open field where we bear left on a footpath round the edge of the field parallel with the road. At the end of the field we go through a gap in the hedge and bear left to cross the A.225 to a stony track opposite taking us over the railway. After about a hundred yards, opposite a track coming in on the left, we turn right on a grassy track which bears slightly left to join another track and then goes forward for about half a mile, later going slightly downhill and finishing as a narrower enclosed path before we finally come out on the road. We turn right and after going under the railway bridge turn left for Shoreham Station.

Knockholt

High Wood, Pratts Bottom. 6 miles

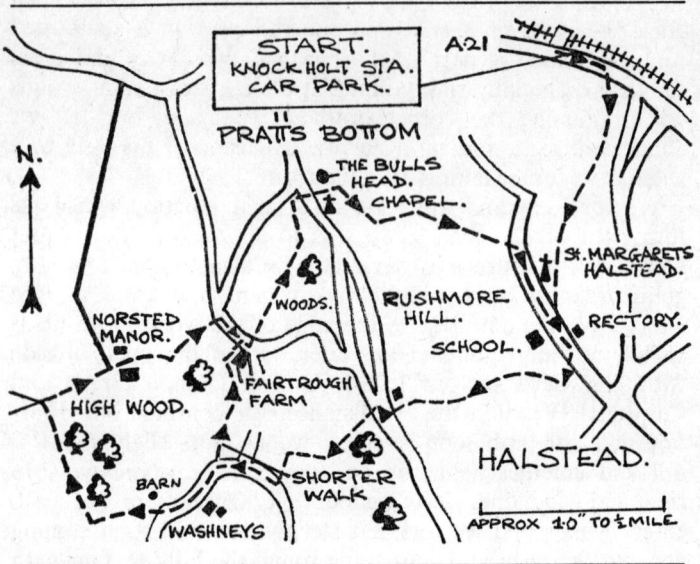

SOME of the paths are likely to be muddy.

How to get there: By train to Knockholt Station or by 402 or 431A bus or Green Line 704. There is a free car park a few yards past Knockholt Station.

From Knockholt Station we turn left down the A.21 for a short distance to a stile and a signposted footpath on the right. We go uphill diagonally left, passing a few free-standing conifers on our left, go forward to a stile under a telegraph pole, over a tarmac drive and along the edge of a field with the hedge on our right. At the end of the field we bear left for a few yards and continue across the centre of the next field on a well defined track. Maintaining direction, we continue through an area of orchards, going over two stiles and finally out through a kissing gate to the road opposite a school.

Turning left down the road for a short distance to just past The Old Rectory on the left we turn right through a gate into the school playing fields and at once bear left parallel with the road to a stile just beyond a white notice board. Once over the stile we bear right downhill on a fairly wide grassy track with a hedge and fence on our right. We are soon in an open area of scrub with a pleasant outlook and continue up the other side of a dip, later levelling out. After another stile an enclosed footpath takes us out to the road with Rushmore Hill Cottage on our right. We cross over and turn right down Hookwood Road, in a few yards turning left over a stile and going forward with the hedge on our left, following the line of telegraph wires. Our path later bears right into a wooded area and goes downhill to a stile and across the bottom of the valley. Another stile takes us uphill into woods and on emerging we turn left with a wire fence and open field on our right. We come out to the road and turn right for 200 yards or so before turning left at a T junction.

We follow this minor road for about a quarter of a mile and as the road bends left we turn right over a patch of grass to a path with an open barn on our right and a narrow belt of woods on our left. Later at a crossing track we turn right going slightly downhill through High Wood. We continue through a more open area crossing the bottom of a valley and bearing right uphill enjoying pleasant aspects. Our path then enters woodland and we soon turn right on a crossing track with a wire fence on our left taking us downhill and out through a kissing gate to the side of an open valley. We cross this diagonally left making for the far left hand corner at the top of the slope, finally going over a stile to a wide track where we turn right uphill for a few yards to a crossing track. Turning left on this track we soon pass on our left Norsted Manor, basically 13th century but much restored, and on our right farm buildings and a row of houses.

Our track, now a surfaced lane, continues with open fields

either side and finally brings us out to a minor road where we turn right uphill. We soon have Fairtrough farm buildings on our right and opposite the farm house we turn left over fields on an enclosed signposted footpath which we follow for about half a mile. Later we have woods on our right and our path goes downhill passing the buildings of Woodhill Farm on our left. We are joined by a drive coming in on the right and continue on past one or two houses out to the road on the outskirts of Pratts Bottom. We turn right to cross a green and another road and take a signposted uphill footpath with a small chapel on the right and The Bulls Head on the left.

When we are nearly at the top of the hill we turn right over a stile and continue over a field to woods ahead. We go over bars into the wood on a well defined path, soon ignoring a right fork. At a crossing track we turn left soon going uphill with a field on our left. On emerging from the wood we continue direction on a field path for about a quarter of a mile finally coming out to a road where we turn right. We soon pass St. Margaret's Church, Halstead, and after about another 100 yards we turn left through a kissing gate.

We are now retracing our steps over the beginning of the walk and we continue on over two stiles, through orchards, over the centre of a field turning left for a few yards before we continue along the edge of the next field. We cross a drive to a stile and continue forward keeping a group of conifers on our right and dropping down slightly left to the stile on the A.21 with an entrance to the free car park opposite and Knockholt Station a short distance away on the left.

Refreshments: Pratts Bottom.

Ightham

Oldbury Hill, Stone Street, Raspit Hill. 6¾ miles
Oldbury Hill, Raspit Hill. 5 miles

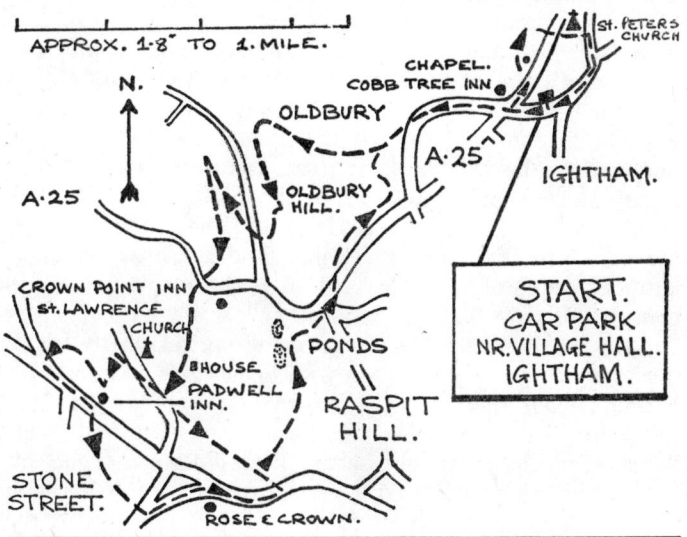

THIS walk gives us a good deal of woodland walking and would be suitably shady for a hot summer's day, while in late spring there will be bluebells and fruit blossom. Above all, it is recommended for autumn when the changing colours of the wooded hillsides and valleys can be seen to full effect. In July there are bilberries in some of the woods and an abundance of sweet chestnuts in October. The walk includes some gentle gradients and only one rather steep path.

How to get there: Maidstone & District buses Nos. 8 and 322. By car on the A.25. Ightam is just off the A.25 about 5½ miles east of Riverhead and there is a free car park next to the village hall.

Turning right out of the car park we are soon out of the

village and cross the A.25 to a side road opposite passing on our right the Cobb Tree Inn. We follow this road for about a third of a mile through the pleasant semi-rural residential area of Oldbury, ignoring a left and a right turning after which the road continues direction as a bridleway. We are soon at The Coach House where we ignore the right fork going uphill and continue direction passing the house on our left and entering woods, mainly sweet chestnut trees. Our path later becomes a gully and gradually goes uphill to a junction of paths at the north east corner of Oldbury Hill.

Oldbury Hill, a National Trust property, was once an Iron Age camp but its antiquarian interest has been largely obscured by the growth of the trees, though the rampart and ditch can be more easily seen at the south end of the hill. Benjamin Harrison (1837–1921) who lived throughout his life in a grocer's shop in Ightham and achieved an international reputation in the field of archaeology picked up many of his stone flints on this hill.

At a junction of paths we take the second on the right, thus keeping slraight on, soon with open fields and orchards visible on our right. After about a quarter of a mile, near the end of the orchards, we are at a junction of several paths, three of which go straight ahead. We take the extreme left hand one of these and after a short distance it turns left with a steep drop on the right. This path takes us round the wooded hillside and soon in a more open area we have fine views across a valley on our right. When we reach a small hollow on the right of the path we turn right dropping down to a stile and going steeply downhill at the side of an enclosed plantation of young beeches. At the bottom of the hill we leave the plantation by means of another stile and turn right on a footpath which soon brings us to the road.

Without going out to the road we turn left on a clear track, keeping parallel with the road, and after about 60 or 70 yards forking right to cross the road to a car parking space. Here we bear right, passing the end of a car parking barrier on our left, and almost at once turning right on a wide bridleway. After 150 yards or so we emerge from the trees into the open and turn sharply left, doubling back, so that we continue with woods on our left and on our right an upward sloping hillside, fairly open, with a few silver birch and, in summer, foxgloves. After about a quarter of a mile, when we are nearly at the main road ahead, audible rather than visible, we turn right for a short distance on a track parallel with the road and go uphill, bearing left to the road verge.

We cross the A.25 to a lay-by, formerly the old road, with Crown Point Inn down on our left, and turn right on a drive by the side of a cottage. We soon have fields on both sides and after about a quarter of a mile we pass a house on our left and go uphill with some fine parkland trees on our right, coming out over a stile to a bridleway.

For the shorter version

We turn left in the bridleway and are soon on a tree lined ridge with an impressive drop on our right, formerly quarries, now somewhat wooded. After about a third of a mile, by some old chestnut paling fencing we turn left downhill.

For the longer version

We turn right in the bridleway soon continuing along a small road and passing on our right a primary school and St. Lawrence's church, a charming little 19th century building well worth a visit.

The road shortly bears right but we continue forward on a track into trees and after some 50 or 60 yards, opposite a small path on the right, we turn sharply left and go downhill on a path which at first is somewhat indistinct but if we keep one or two large beech trees on our left we will find the path becomes clearer lower down. Nearer the bottom of the hill we turn right on a crossing track and continue on through pleasant open woodland for about a quarter of a mile. Our track then enters an area of chestnut trees and bears right slightly uphill. Without going uphill we take a path branching off on the left towards a chestnut paling fence where we bear left, with the fence and later a house visible through trees on our right. Our path soon merges into the house drive and we continue to a minor road where we turn left, in a few yards turning left again on another road.

We are soon passing on our left a few houses on the out-skirts of Stone Street and The Padwell Inn, opposite which we turn right on a signposted footpath taking us over fields with orchards on our right. Ignoring paths branching off we keep to the main track and after rather less than half a mile are out at a road junction.

We now have half a mile of road walking and have the choice of taking the first road on the left which will enable us to see something of Stone Street, turning right at the T junction, but adds another 200 yards or so of road walking, or taking the second fork on the left which later joins the road coming from Stone Street at The Rose and Crown.

We continue past the inn and just after passing Greens Cottages on the left we may if desired obtain access to the extensive disused sand quarries which are a spectacular sight, and are well worth exploring. Retracing our steps to the road, a little further along, opposite a stony downhill track turning off on the right we turn left uphill on a small path among trees, ignoring a left fork and continuing steeply up-hill soon with a precipitous drop to the old quarry on our left. Our path flattens out and we continue with fine views across the quarry on our left and a drop on our right also. By some broken chestnut paling fencing on our right we turn right downhill under some large beech trees.

Both walks now follow the same route

We continue forward on a main bridleway through pleasant open woods for about half a mile, with the slopes of Raspit Hill on our right, and rising ground on our left forming a wide valley. The last part of this track takes us past a string of small ponds on our left in an area known as Fish Ponds Wood. Especially when the ponds are full after a wet season they make a pleasant spot in which to linger.

When we are about 100 yards short of the main road ahead we take a right fork, soon turning right again in open woods among bracken. We cross a wider path and continue

56

on a somewhat rising path soon taking another small path on our left out to the road A.25 which we cross to an uphill track slightly to our right. This track follows the road at first at a higher level then bears left and has embankments either side. After a few yards we turn right on some steps up the embankment and continue forward on a wide track under trees taking us round the east side of Oldbury Hill. After half a mile our path bears left and we maintain direction across an open glade. After 100 yards or so we finally come out at a junction of paths which may look familiar as we were here earlier in the walk. Avoiding the first path on the right, which was the gully we came up earlier, we take the second path on the right and soon have an open field visible on our left. Another small path feeds in on the left and we are shortly at a small clearing where we bear slightly right on a path keeping a small gully on our left. With embankments either side our path goes downhill, down a few stone steps and continues with a house soon visible through trees on our right.

We are soon out by The Coach House and continue along the bridleway and the road through Oldbury, thus retracing an early part of the walk. When we reach the Cobb Tree Inn we bear left round it to the old road and go forward parallel with the main road, bearing left at a chapel, but not taking the path at the side of the chapel. We soon bear right with house gardens on our right and after sloping uphill and then downhill we turn right on an enclosed path through cultivations, finally turning left up to the road. We cross diagonally right to a downhill sloping path, soon turning left on an enclosed path and up some steps into the churchyard of St. Peter's Church, Ightham. Parts of the existing church date back to Norman times and it contains the 14th century tomb of Sir Thomas Cawne.

Leaving the church we turn right downhill continuing direction through Ightham village, passing several inns and beautiful timbered houses. Keeping to the pavement on the right we pass some shops and are soon back at the car park by the village hall.

Refreshment: Stone Street and Ightham.

Knole Park

**Ightham Mote, Wilmot Hill, One Tree Hill, Carters Hill.
8 miles.
Knole Park, One Tree Hill, Carters Hill. 6 miles.
Godden Green, Ightham Mote, Wilmot Hill, One Tree Hill.
6¼ miles.**

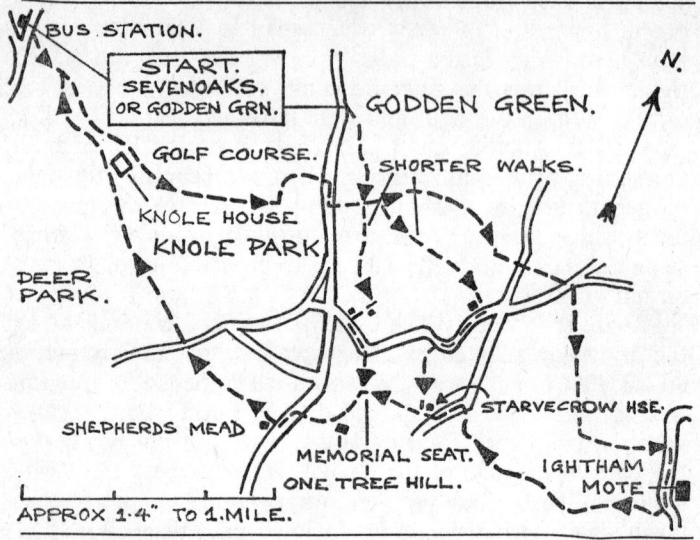

HERE we have plenty of variety: pleasant woodland and parkland walking, with herds of deer to be seen in Knole Park, hillside walking with views, orchards in blossom in late spring and historic buildings of great beauty and antiquity. This is a suitable walk for any time of the year.

This is an 8 mile walk starting from Sevenoaks and going to Ightham Mote and back, but if Knole Park is omitted the walk can be started from the village of Godden Green and the walk to Ightham Mote and back is then 6¼ miles.

How to get there: Many different buses serve Sevenoaks and there are several free car parks near Knole Park. A 98 bus from Sevenoaks will take us to Godden Green village.

Turning right out of the east side of Sevenoaks bus station, just past the pedestrian crossing we turn left down Buckhurst Lane with a car park on the right at the end of which we cross another car park diagonally right to join a footpath leading down to Knole Park. After a kissing gate our path takes us forward and uphill among a few trees, and we continue direction over a tarmac drive on a less clearly defined path. We are on a small hill known as Echo Mount and after passing a hollow on the left the buildings of Knole come into sight ahead on the right.

This vast and historic house was originally built in the 15th century as a palace for the Archbishops of Canterbury and greatly extended early in the 17th century. Since Tudor times it has belonged to the Sackville family and is now in the care of The National Trust. It is open to the public March—November, admission 50p.

Continuing down the grassy slope, we keep the side of the house on our right and just after the end of the buildings we bear left over the grass on a clear path taking us over a golf course. We continue forward over two successive crossing tracks and a tarmac path, after which we go down a dip and up the other side, keeping to the main track on the left. At the top of the hill we pass a small pond on our right and continue forward, soon going downhill to a gate stile and bearing left past two cottages into a wooded area.

Just past a crossing track we turn right through a kissing gate, go diagonally left across a field to another kissing gate, then forward and slightly right to a stile and the road. Here we turn right and, after passing the first house on the left, we turn left down a drive marked "Little Steading". We are soon on a footpath enclosed at first, later with a fence on the left and when this ends we continue direction into pleasant open woodland, Lord's Spring Wood. Later at a well defined crossing track we turn right and we now have the choice of the longer or shorter versions.

For the shorter version

We continue along this track later going slightly downhill and over a stile taking us out of Lord's Spring Wood. A wide grassy enclosed path soon takes us uphill, flattens out and then takes us gently downhill to two stiles. Once over these we go uphill again into woods and our path flattens and becomes a drive which we follow till, with a house on our right, we come out on the road. We turn right for about quarter of a mile and soon after the road bends sharply right at a telegraph pole we turn left into woods known as Bitchet Common. We go over a crossing track and continue direction soon with an open field visible on the left. Later we maintain direction over a drive leading to Starvecrow House which is visible across the field on our left. When we have come rather less than half a mile from the road the field on our left ends at a junction of paths and we keep straight ahead to the National Trust sign and slightly uphill through the wooded area of One Tree Hill.

For the longer version

We walk along the track for about 50 yards and then turn left on a clear path, finally coming out on a rough drive where we turn right. After passing a house on the left we continue downhill on a small footpath, later bearing right with woods on our left. We pass a farm on the left and bear slightly right on a rough track to the road which we cross to a signposted footpath taking us over fields with orchards on the left. When we come to a road we again cross to a footpath opposite. This time it is a wide track between orchards which we follow for about half a mile, keeping right when it forks. Eventually, after passing some overgrown brick walls on the left our path bears left downhill into Broadhoath Wood. Another track also bears left at this point but we take the righthand one. After continuing downhill through pleasant woodland, among abundant bluebells in late spring, our path turns left and here, if desired, we may make a short but interesting diversion into the trees on our right to trace the spring which is the source of the stream now flowing alongside our path. We continue forward, using mud avoidance paths on the left if necessary, and when the woods on the left give way to a field, we have the option of remaining on our path or using a parallel path just inside the woods on our right: there is an opening in the woods taking us over the stream just opposite the start of the field.

The parallel path later rejoins the original track and we continue out to the road where we turn right soon coming in sight of the rear of Ightham Mote on our left. This picturesque half-timbered manor house dates from 1340 and has been beautifully restored by its present owner. It is open to the public on Friday afternoons throughout the year and most Bank Holidays, admission 25p.

We pass on our left a row of charming Tudor cottages which were formerly a stable block of Ightham Mote and the road bears left to the gates of the house. Fortunately for us a public footpath goes in front of the house so we turn down the drive and are able to get a good sight of the house, surrounded by its wide moat, fed by springs, set in exquisite gardens. Retracing our steps to the entrance gates, we turn right for a few yards then left through the buildings of Mote Farm, soon turning right again on a rough slightly rising track which we follow for about a mile. Later this track flattens somewhat and at a footpath sign we turn right with fields on our left. We continue up the gradual slope of Wilmot Hill enjoying wide views on our left: the South Downs are visible on a clear day. For most of the way we have enclosed woods on our right and at one point our path goes down a dip and up again. When the top of the hill is reached we turn right, passing an orchard on our left before reaching the road.

We cross to a bridleway opposite, turning left in woods and following the line of the road, with a good deal of twisting to avoid mud. The path soon bears right, away from the road, and we continue through pleasant open woods keeping near the edge of the wood which is mainly on our right. Our path goes downhill and we pass Starvecrow House in a clearing on our right before going uphill and at the corner of a field on our right turning left at a National Trust sign on a main path through the wooded area of One Tree Hill.

Both walks now follow the same route

We reach a stone memorial seat at the top of the escarpment and after admiring the fine view to the south we turn right downhill, go through a rustic barrier and continue along the hillside. We finally go through another barrier and downhill to the road.

We turn left downhill for a short distance before taking a drive on the right to a house named Shepherds Mead and immediately turning right on an enclosed footpath leading into woods. We go over a stile and continue along the edge of woods on Carter's Hill for about a quarter of a mile when we go over a stile to a crossing track, turn right uphill for a few yards then left over another stile into a field. We continue direction along the side of the field with the hedge on our left, turning right at the corner of the field and watching carefully for a stile on the left, partly obscured by bushes, which will take us into woods. Once over the stile we go straight forward, ignoring paths on the left and right and are soon out on the road which we cross to a kissing gate opposite, leading into the grounds of Knole Park.

Going forward through an area of beech we cross Chestnut Walk and continue direction on a surfaced path. Later, after passing nursery buildings over on our right, we cross a tarmac drive and keep forward and right on a grassy path taking us towards the wall enclosing the gardens of Knole. We continue forward under trees with the wall on our right, enjoying pleasant views on our left and at one point a fine view of Knole itself on our right. As the wall ends we turn diagonally right keeping a valley on our left and making for some trees ahead. We bear right over two successive tarmac paths and reach the drive leading to the house, continuing on this for 100 yards or so with Echo Mount on your right. At a crossing drive we turn right for a short distance taking the first track on the left. This goes downhill among trees finally bringing us to the kissing gate and path leading uphill to the car park. We retrace our steps to the main road where we turn right and are soon back at the bus station and car park.

Godden Green, Ightham Mote, Wilmot Hill, One Tree Hill

From Riverhead we go eastwards along the A.25 for 2½ miles to Seal, turning right at the cross roads for just over a mile to the village of Godden Green, where there is a small car parking area on the green.

Passing The Bucks Head Inn on our right we bear left on a tarmac drive with a notice indicating that it leads to Mary's Mead Holiday Home. This later becomes a bridleway taking us past a few large houses and after a third of a mile we go under a bar on our right into woods, continuing with a fence on our right. After about 200 yards the fence turns right but we turn left on a track into Lord's Spring Wood, a pleasant open woodland, later turning right at a well defined crossing track.

We now follow the longer version to One Tree Hill.

We reach the stone memorial seat at the top of the escarpment and after admiring the fine view to the south we retrace our steps to The National Trust sign. We are now back at the junction of paths and with the corner of the wire fence on our right we bear left downhill and forward on a pleasant path through open woodland along the bottom of a small valley. When we come out on the road we turn left and soon go uphill, turning right on a drive at the top of the hill with Fawke Farm House on our left. We pass another house on our right and continue forward, ignoring a left fork. As we approach some barns ahead we turn left on a rutted lane which bears right, passing a house on our left. Opposite a bungalow we turn right over a bar stile at the side of a gate and cross a field to another stile ahead. We cross the next field bearing slightly left to the corner of a hedge and continue forward with the hedge on our right. On reaching the corner of the field we cross a stile and continue direction slightly uphill with a sweet chestnut plantation on our left and good views on our right.

Later we come to the corner of a wooden fence on our left and we maintain direction with the fence on our left. We are now retracing our steps over the beginning part of the walk and when the fence ends we go under a bar and turn left on a track, continuing on past one or two large houses for about a third of a mile till we come out on to the green of Godden Green Village.

Refreshment: Sevenoaks, Godden Green.

Leigh

**Penshurst, Penshurst Place. 7¼ miles.
Leigh, Penshurst Park. 5 miles.**

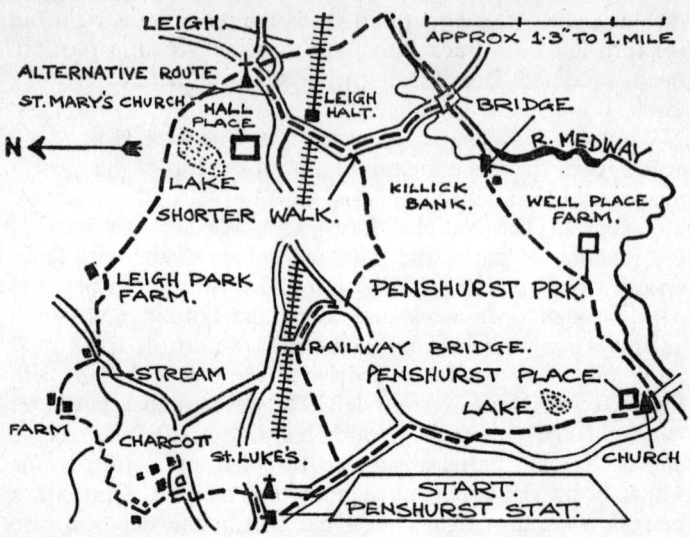

THIS is a beautiful parkland and farmland walk with fine expansive views. There are only the gentlest of gradients and the walk is suitable for summer as there is likely to be a considerable amount of mud in the wetter months. It is well worth enduring a certain amount of mud to enjoy the spectacular colours of autumn.

How to get there: By train to Penshurst station where there is a car park. By 233 or 234 bus (Maidstone & District).

Leaving Penshurst Station on the north side we turn right up the road soon passing St. Luke's Church on the right and immediately turning left on an enclosed footpath over fields. Coming out to a road we turn right for a short distance then left on a small road which bears right to the hamlet of

Charcott and The Greyhound Inn while we continue direction on a lane taking us into farm buildings. At a pond on the left we turn right through a gate passing an ancient house on the right, and soon going through a gate on a track with the field hedge over on our left. Another gate takes us into the next field where we turn right with the hedge on our right following its twists and turns until we reach a bridge on the right taking us over a stream. We continue forward with the hedge still on our right. After a bar stile into the next field we bear diagonally left uphill towards Wickhurst Farm, go through a metal gate with a barn on our left and turn right on a lane passing farm buildings on our right.

We continue down the lane between fields for about a quarter of a mile coming out to the road with picturesque Copping Brook Cottages on our left. Crossing to a plank bridge over a stream, we turn left along the edge of a field at first keeping parallel with the road which later bears away from us. We continue with the hedge on our left, enjoying pleasant aspects on the right. At the end of the field we go over a bar stile and turn right on a surfaced lane leading to Leigh Park Farm. Just past a pond and some oast houses we turn right into a field, keeping the hedge on our left and continuing through two more fields before going over a stile into pleasant mixed woodlands. After another stile our path continues along the edge of the grounds of Hall Place with a fence on the right and the lake and shrubberies soon visible beyond. The path ends at a kissing gate where we turn right in a field with a fence on our right, soon passing the house, a Tudor style mansion built in 1871-2. After another field we come out to the road between a lodge and gate house of Hall Place. Here we may make an optional diversion by turning right through the churchyard to visit the church. Some parts of St. Mary's Church, Leigh, date back to the 13th century but most of the present walls were rebuilt and the tower completed in the middle of the 19th century.

Turning right down the road we are soon at the picturesque village of Leigh with its large village green, shop, toilets and several inns affording opportunity for refreshment. As the village ends, we take the first turning on the left, signposted to Bidborough, soon going under the railway bridge at Leigh Halt and going uphill past oasthouses.

For the shorter version

As the road flattens at a house named Pauls Hill we turn right on a signposted footpath taking us into Penshurst Place Estate. After a squeeze stile we continue direction on a track which soon gives us good views on both sides. Soon after passing two small ponds on the right our track, now barely visible, forks and we bear slightly left, continuing along a splendid and very wide avenue of plane trees and enjoying good views on the right from our relatively high position. After about a quarter of a mile we go through a gate with a stile, still continuing direction on a wide track, which is very muddy in winter.

The avenue ends and we finally go through a squeeze stile and turn right through another squeeze stile thus doubling back somewhat. We are now on a pleasant grassy track between conifer plantations and continue direction over a wide crossing track, finally going slightly downhill to a wooden gate and squeeze stile. This gives us access to an enclosed path which goes slightly uphill till, at a wooden hut, we bear left to another stile. We cross this and turn left down a grassy path with conifers on our right, soon bearing left downhill and out to the road.

After turning left for a few yards we turn right on a corner cutting path and continue along a pleasant lane for about a quarter of a mile, turning left with the lane. On our right we pass a bridge over the railway and maintain direction on a track parallel with the railway at first, later going through a gate with a footpath sign and keeping along the side of a field with the hedgerow on our left. We continue through two more fields with a hopfield on our right and woods on the left, coming out through the buildings of Moorden Farm to the road. We turn right down to the fork and take the lane on the left back to the timber yard and Penshurst Station.

For the longer version

Continuing down the road for about half a mile we come to the bridge over the River Medway and turn right over a stile before the road crosses the bridge.

We follow the river on our left through pleasant riverside scenery, later going through a squeeze stile and continuing forward bearing right to a bridge over a tributary. Once over the bridge we bear slightly left uphill passing on our left Killick's Bank, a pleasant house and cottage. Our path is now a cart track and bears right uphill with the hedge on our left. As we gradually gain height we can enjoy splendid views on all sides and finally at the top of the hill we go through a gate and forward, passing on our left the end of an avenue of trees leading down to Well Place Farm. We now go down-hill, bearing slightly left and making for a large free-standing lime tree, beyond which is a stile in the lower corner of the field. After crossing the stile we go forward for a short distance along the edge of the field then bear left over bars into a surfaced lane where we turn right. We continue on this lane for over half a mile, soon sighting Penshurst Place ahead on our right and come out under an arched gate to the road. We go forward for a few yards before turning right up some steps into the picturesque courtyard leading into the churchyard of the Penshurst Church, but before doing this we can make an optional diversion into the village of Pens-hurst where there are shops for teas and ices, an inn and toilets.

The exterior of the church is largely 19th century, but parts of the interior date back to the 13th and 14th centuries. Continuing through the churchyard past the church we go through a kissing gate into Penshurst Park, passing Penshurst Place on our right and crossing the drive through squeeze stiles. As we keep forward the lake comes into sight on our right and after crossing a stile in a chestnut paling fence we go gradually uphill towards woods ahead. At the corner of the woods we maintain direction with the woods on our left, enjoying fine views on our right. At the top of the hill we can look back at Penshurst Place about half a mile away in its beautiful parkland setting and we turn left on a small path with a fence on the right bringing us out to the road where we turn right. We are soon at a road junction where we turn left down the road signposted to Penshurst Station. After passing Moorden Farm on the right we continue along the lane on the left to Penshurst Station.

To avoid a certain amount of road walking for the longer version there is a pleasant alternative route through water meadows to the Medway bridge during the summer only. The track at one point is impassably muddy in winter.

Coming from Leigh Church we cross the village green going down Green View Avenue and over a stile to a hedge lined track which takes us under a railway bridge. We continue direction over a field with the hedge on our right, go through a gate and across the next field on a faintly visible track, making for a bridge ahead in trees and enjoying pleasant aspects. After crossing the River Medway we turn left for about 20 yards then right over another bridge and forward on a track, soon going through a squeeze stile at the side of a metal gate. We turn right in the field for a few yards to a plank bridge and another squeeze stile. The river is hidden in trees on our right and we continue forward for about a third of a mile, going through two more squeeze stiles, till we finally come out to the road at the side of a gate. We turn right crossing the Medway on a bridge and immediately turn left over a stile.

Refreshment: Charcott, Leigh and Penshurst.

Hever

Markbeech, Hill Hoath. 6 miles.

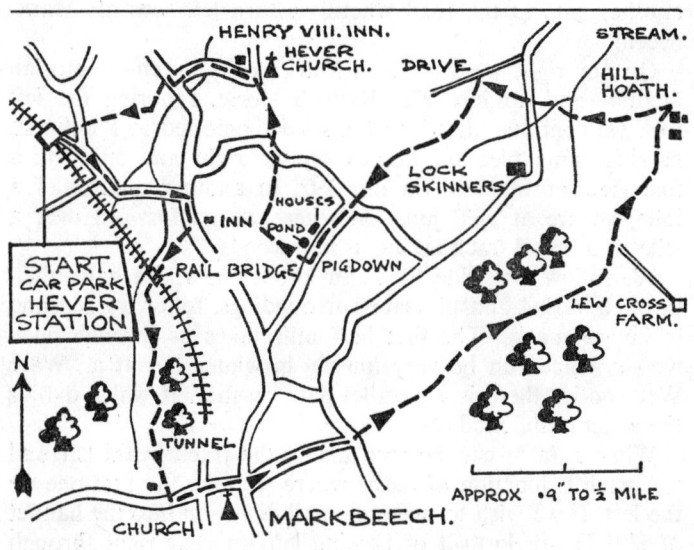

THIS walk will enable those already familiar with Hever Castle to explore the pleasant woods and fields in the vicinity and see the path through the rock cleft at Hill Hoath. This would be suitable for hot weather as there are no hills and a good deal of the walk is in shady woodland. It will be very muddy in winter.

How to get there: By train to Hever Station where there is a car park.

Leaving Hever Station we bear right up the station approach road, with a fine view on the left, turning right in the road, passing a turning on the right and going downhill to cross two streams. At a T junction we turn right on the road signposted to Markbeech and soon turn right on a footpath at the side of a bungalow. Our path takes us under a railway bridge and turns left uphill with a wire fence on the right, later continuing direction into woods. After about a quarter of a mile the wood ends and we bear slightly left on an enclosed footpath, through a gate with a house on the right, then along the side of a paddock and out through another gate to the road where we turn left towards Markbeech.

On our right we soon pass Markbeech church—Victorian Gothic—and an inn, The Kentish Horse. Ignoring the left fork we continue ahead on the road signposted to Penshurst, passing some pleasant houses on the right and enjoying a fine view of Ide Hill on our left. In another quarter of a mile we are at a T junction where we go forward over a stile on a broad track taking us into woods.

We follow this wide track for about one and a half miles, through varied and pleasant surroundings, following red and white waymarks. The first half mile takes us through open woods which can be very muddy in winter but at a "Ware Wet" notice there is a parallel path on the left which avoids the worst of the mud.

When a farm can be seen ahead the track bears left and we reach a junction of paths where we take the first one on the left. If we wish to make a small diversion into the hamlet of Hill Hoath instead of turning left we bear right through a gate, passing a beautiful timbered house. Retracing our steps through the gate we continue on, ignoring a main turning on the right.

Our path takes us into woods and is decidedly muddy in winter. Very soon we have steep embankments on either side and the path then goes through a deep cutting in the sandstone rocks entwined with tree roots. This rock area is quite spectacular and well worth further exploration: on the left there is a parallel path at the top of the cutting, which also avoids the mud.

After we emerge from the cutting there is a path along the top of the embankment on the right which may be used as an alternative: this takes us under some beech trees and both paths join later and continue as a grassy track with a clearing on the left. We then take a left fork continuing along

70

the well defined track and when the path goes down a hollow we turn right over a plank bridge and stile and continue along the side of a field with the woods on our right. At the corner of the field we go through a gate and turn left up the side of a crop field with the hedge on our left, finally coming out to the road. We cross to a signposted footpath and go slightly uphill under a few tall conifers keeping the fence on our left.

Passing a bungalow on our left we come out to a drive and immediately turn left over a stile to an enclosed footpath which takes us into a field where we go forward with the hedge on our right. We continue direction along the edge of two more fields, at the corner of the third one turning left with trees and fence on our right and out through a gate to a road junction. We take the road ahead signposted to Markbeech and Cowden, later passing a few cottages and a pond on our right.

Just past the last cottage we turn right on a signposted footpath crossing the field diagonally right to a stile a few yards to the right of a five-barred gate in the corner. After crossing the stile we turn right and continue with the hedge on our right enjoying views of Toy's Hill and Ide Hill ahead. We go over a double stile in the corner of the field and maintain direction with woods on our right. At the next corner of the field we take a stile hidden in the trees, just left of a telegraph pole. This brings us to an open field where we bear right towards the spire of Hever church in the distance. After a short distance we take a stile on the right into a belt of trees and go down a short path to the road. We turn left for a few yards before turning right on a signposted and surfaced footpath taking us past a school and out to the road at Hever opposite the Henry VIII Inn.

The church on our right dates back in part to Norman times and if we wish to visit the 14th century Hever Castle, once the home of Anne Boleyn, the entrance is just past the church on the right. (Open to the public on Bank Holidays and Sundays, Wednesdays and Fridays in the summer months 1–7 p.m. Admission to Castle 35p. To gardens only 25p.)

Retracing our steps we turn right downhill with the inn on

our right passing a pleasant thatched cottage, going over a stream and continuing to a T junction where we turn right. In a few yards we turn left on a signposted footpath and just before a stile we turn right through the hedge and under a bar to a field where we go forward and uphill to the corner of some woods ahead, or, if crops are growing, bear left round the field. On reaching the corner of the woods we bear left, thus circling round somewhat to a stile under some trees, passing a small pond on our right. Once over the stile we go forward to a gate ahead, passing another pond on the right, and continue direction on a visible track with the hedgerow on our right, enjoying pleasant aspects on the left. Another stile brings us out to the road where we turn right for a few yards and left up Hever Station approach road.

Refreshment: Markbeech and Hever.